Palgrave Studies in Animals and Social Problems

Series Editor
Leslie Irvine
Department of Sociology
University of Colorado Boulder
Boulder, CO, USA

Because other species make up the economic, sociological, emotional, and moral fabric of society, they play important roles in countless social problems. Some criminal activities have connections to animal abuse and fighting. Income inequality and discrimination have historically influenced pet prohibitions in rental housing by disproportionately affecting residents with low incomes. Confined livestock operations, animal hoarding, dog bites, and zoonotic disease transmission have public health and environmental implications. Wildlife poaching and the illegal traffic in endangered species threaten conservation efforts and defy international law. Because animals lack voices and social power, they cannot attract attention to the social problems that involve them. Incorporating animals into the study of social problems provides a clearer understanding of what groups and individuals consider problematic, how problems emerge on the social landscape, and what solutions might address them. This series transforms the scholarly analysis of social problems by focusing on how animals contribute to and suffer from issues long considered uniquely human. For further information on the series and submitting your work, please get in touch with Leslie Irvine (University of Colorado Boulder, USA) at Leslie.Irvine@Colorado.edu.

More information about this series at
http://www.palgrave.com/gp/series/15441

Nik Taylor • Heather Fraser

Companion Animals and Domestic Violence

Rescuing Me, Rescuing You

Nik Taylor
University of Canterbury
Christchurch, New Zealand

Heather Fraser
School of Public Health and Social Work
Queensland University of Technology
Kelvin Grove, QLD, Australia

Palgrave Studies in Animals and Social Problems
ISBN 978-3-030-04124-3   ISBN 978-3-030-04125-0   (eBook)
https://doi.org/10.1007/978-3-030-04125-0

Library of Congress Control Number: 2018963558

Cover illustration: © fabio camandona / Alamy Stock Photo

This Palgrave Macmillan imprint is published by the registered company Springer Nature Switzerland AG
The registered company address is: Gewerbestrasse 11, 6330 Cham, Switzerland

This book is dedicated to all victims/survivors of domestic violence—
irrespective of species.

Acknowledgements

We would like to thank all the participants of the studies that informed this book. For the *Loving You* project, this includes the women and their animal companions who greeted us so warmly when we visited them at home—Julie Felus and Carley Milich from the Northern Domestic Violence Service in South Australia; and Celine Graham from Relationships Australia (SA, North). Special recognition needs to go to Julie Felus for creating pet-friendly women's refuge possibilities over the last decade. We would also like to acknowledge Damien Riggs, our friend and colleague, who was a key part of some of the projects mentioned in this book and who also prompted us to think differently about some of our ideas.

Thanks also to Naomi Stekelenburg from Queensland University of Technology (QUT) for helping with the editing prior to manuscript submission, and to all at Palgrave for your patience and support.

Nik would like to thank, as always, the furry folk in her household: Squirt, Loki, and Bailey. They remind her why this work is important, help her through the bad days, and provide a constant source of laughter.

Heather would like to thank Bruce (human partner), Alice (Bernese Mountain Dog), Murray (ginger collie-kelpie rescue), Gus (wire-haired Border Terrier), Sunny (ginger fluffy stray cat), and Charli (white patchy moggie) for their joyful and life-affirming support. She also remembers with love the dog from her childhood, called Teeny, and the cats, Fluffy, Cobber, Boney, and Boney Jnr.

Contents

1 Human and Animal Victims of Domestic Violence: Being
  Rescued   3

2 The Links In-and-Between Human-Animal Abuses: Love,
  Loyalty, and Pain   29

3 What We Choose to Hear: Researching Human-Animal
  Violence   59

4 Being Subjected to Domestic Violence: Empathic Love and
  Domination   93

5 Foregrounding Companion Animals' Experiences of
  Domestic Violence   123

6 Supporting Victims/Survivors: Escape, Refuge, and
  Recovery   155

7   The Work of Significant Other/s: Companion Animal
    Relationships in the Future   187

Index   219

List of Figures

Fig. 1.1   Woman with cat on shoulder   1
Fig. 1.2   Conceptual model relating individual, social, and ecological
            factors to intimate partner violence. (Beyer et al. 2015)   19
Fig. 2.1   Woman with terrier on knee   27
Fig. 3.1   Woman with a white bull terrier   57
Fig. 4.1   Black cat   91
Fig. 5.1   Tortoiseshell cat   121
Fig. 6.1   Woman hugging dog   153
Fig. 7.1   Woman watching cat on floor   185

Fig. 1.1 Woman with cat on shoulder

1

Human and Animal Victims of Domestic Violence: Being Rescued

Introduction

Domestic violence is a serious social problem across the world that has short- and long-term effects on individuals dominated and violated by trusted 'loved ones' (García-Moreno et al. 2005; Garcia-Moreno and Watts 2011). Beyond this, it also negatively impacts more than the immediate victims targeted and/or directly exposed to it. Extended families, local communities, and whole societies are impacted not only by the injuries that are caused—visible and hidden—but also by the estimated economic losses, such as lost days at work or the cost of healthcare to treat the injured (AIHW 2018; García-Moreno et al. 2005; Garcia-Moreno and Watts 2011). While not all injuries are permanent, many are; and in many places including the UK, the US, Canada, Australia, and many European countries, homicides from domestic violence occur at least weekly (AIHW 2018; NCADV 2018; Statistics Canada 2016). For companion animals, however, domestic violence carries additional risks, such as being killed by human perpetrators of violence, often without any redress or public scrutiny; being left with violent perpetrators when human victims flee; and the very real possibility of being sent to an animal

© The Author(s) 2019   3
N. Taylor, H. Fraser, *Companion Animals and Domestic Violence*, Palgrave Studies in
Animals and Social Problems, https://doi.org/10.1007/978-3-030-04125-0_1

shelter for fostering and adoption but picked up by a new human 'owner' and the possibility of forced euthanasia, even if rescued (see Patronek 1997). The main aims of this book are to (1) draw attention to the link between domestic violence and animal abuse, (2) take seriously the abuse (and neglect) companion animals can experience in domestic settings, and (3) more widely explore human-companion animal relations. In particular, we move beyond those mainstream discourses that stress the importance of acknowledging animal abuse largely, or solely, in order to recognise and address human-to-human abuse. One part of this is considering more-than-physical-violence harms done to animals experiencing domestic abuse. Another part is recognising how integral positive human-animal relations are to those (human and other species) trying to recover from domestic violence.

Our intention is to represent human-animal relationships in not only accurate but also dignifying ways. This calls for us to go beyond recounting the benefits humans can derive from companion animals as if animals were machines or commodities to be used and discarded. Focusing on the interconnectedness between humans (mostly women) and animals, we ask questions about interspecies reciprocity, mutuality, and welfare in the contexts of domestic domination, control, and violation. As a result, the central themes of this book are rescue, refuge, and recovery, in relation to human and animal victims/survivors' experiences of domestic violence. Yet, this book is as much about emotional connections and empathic love, as it is about seeking rescue and refuge from domestic violence. As we will show, interspecies companionate relationships of connection and love can be life sustaining. For more than a few caught up in domestic violence, these relationships can literally provide victims/survivors with the will to live, eat, sleep, and keep caring for others, and in the process, maintain the will to rebuild their lives.

As we will explain, it is a misconstruction to view companion animal relationships as unidirectional. Most do not flow from human to animal or vice versa. Instead, they are circular, flowing between human and animal and back again in a loop that is consistently reinforced through constant, caring, and empathic interactions. These interactions involve physical touch and proximity, non-verbal and verbal interactions, and an awareness of and curiosity about difference. In contrast to conventional portraits of 'pet ownership,' they may be founded on empathy and not based on assumptions about animals' inferiority. We call these *empathic connections*. In this book, empathic connections are emotionally attuned interactions between humans and other animals that depend upon and promote emotional closeness, physical touch, care of self and other, and an awareness of each other's needs that may be different from our own. With these connections come feelings of rescue, refuge, and sanctuary.

As we explore in Chap. 4, when we speak of *empathic love* between humans and animals we are referring to ongoing, loving companionate relationships that are based on mutual regard and care, emotional attunement, and reciprocal responsiveness to each other's interests and welfare. Empathic love may also include alliances of solidarity, and not just emotional connection. These alliances may be the result of empathic connections, often forged by sharing domestic space together, which can engender some powerful entanglements, particularly in the context of domestic violence, where the power inequalities between humans and animals may be even more accentuated. Even so, an important part of this book is to draw attention to the asymmetrical power relationships that humans and companion animals can experience in the contexts of domestic abuse. By drawing attention to the negative effects domestic violence can have for companion animals, not just humans, we show how companion animals can be victims of domestic violence in their own right.

We use ideas from feminist intersectionality to recognise the potential interconnections between love and abuse, and gender and species. As we explain in Chaps. 3 and 7, our use of intersectionality focuses mostly on the intersections of species, gender, class, and sexuality. Because of the depth and richness of data from one of our projects in particular—the *Loving You, Loving Me* interviews (see Chap. 3 for a detailed outline)—we spend most time providing a close-up examination of nine women's reported experiences of domestic violence by abusive male spouses, along with focusing on the experiences of their companion animals. These stories are used for illustrative purposes, with the narrative details providing fine-grained understandings of how violence can take hold in domestic settings and be hard to recognise, dislodge, seek help for, and obtain some form of socio-cultural redress. Emblematic of the women's stories are the themes of relationships, rescue, refuge, and recovery. As the book unfolds, these themes provide useful ways to consider the wider questions about the politics of domination and the construction of family and significant others.

We hope that this book will be a useful resource for those in domestic violence policy making, service provision and beyond, to draw on when making the case for the establishment of services that enable human and animal victims of domestic violence the opportunity to remain together. We also hope it will inspire more research and different forms of service provision that recognise the needs of animals caught up in domestic violence.

Nevertheless, a few caveats are in order. It is not our aim to suggest that it is only women—cisgender and heterosexual women—who are at risk of being subjected to domestic violence. It has now been well established that domestic violence negatively affects a diverse range of groups, across gender, sexuality, class, ethnicity, age, and, as we will explore, species. Highlighting what animals mean to a small group of mostly heterosexual Australian women in domestic violence situations is just one part of a much broader suite of projects, programmes, and campaigns needed to advance collective understanding and prevention of domestic violence. Many other projects are being undertaken, and yet more still need to be initiated, to address and prevent violence against all groups, across age, genders, sexualities, and other categories of difference (e.g., children, men, women, transgender people, and others). Work taken to prevent and redress violence with victims who are also perpetrators of abuse is equally important. Anger management work, behaviour change programmes, and other attempts to intervene in domestic violence all have a place in the collective efforts to stem and prevent domestic violence. Many other projects and possibilities could be mentioned. Our point is that we recognise that domestic violence has many possibilities, 'or faces,' and many complexities. It is not just something that happens to heterosexual women, and certainly not as passive victims with masochistic tendencies. But it is something that happens to many heterosexual women and, by extension, their companion animals, which is the focus of our book.

As we will show later in this book, several studies have shown that it is common for many victims of domestic violence to remain in violent situations for fear of their animals' safety and well-being. We also know that for those who do end up fleeing without their animals, additional guilt and fear are likely (see Chaps. 2 and 6 for more information). Much less considered is the depth of the connection between human and companion animal victims throughout these experiences. In particular, we have insufficient knowledge about how human-animal connections can help both human and animal trauma victims try to heal in the aftermath of the violence. This is a driving force for the book. Highlighting these deep, emotional interspecies connections and the benefits they can produce for both is one way to advocate for services that protect both human and animal victims of domestic violence. By focusing on the animals, and on the bond between human and animal victims, it may also be a more engaging and effective way to engage the wider public in serious and informed discussions of domestic violence.

While domestic violence is more commonly discussed in public than it was historically, there are still several serious misnomers about it. Many people, for example, still feel it is a 'private' issue that occurs in the home, and few people have a real sense of the daily fear and terror involved for those who are victims of domestic violence. In part, this is a result of it being a difficult and emotional issue to discuss, one that—like animal abuse—is much easier to turn away from. However, we need to dispel existing myths about it if we are to truly address the staggering ubiquity of its practice (see Chap. 2). The first step in achieving this, as those who so courageously highlighted its existence several decades ago pointed out (e.g., Pizzey 1974), is to make it a public, not private, issue. That means we need to engage people about the topic. This isn't easy to do but a focus on the animal victims, and on the positive aspects of our relationships with other animals in post-abuse situations, is, we think, likely to engage all sorts of people who would normally turn away from the issues.

Working on the various projects that form the basis of this book, which we sketch shortly and detail in Chap. 3, has brought the personal experiences both of us had with domestic violence into full view and has, in some ways, added to the already existing challenges of doing work in this area. It has also given us a deeper understanding of the emotions wrought in our participants when they recounted aspects of their abuse while talking to us. And it has ensured that we remain committed to spreading the word about links between domestic violence and animal abuse far and wide—both within and without scholarly publications. Engaging others in the fight for change means first reaching them and, often, prying their eyes open to the realities of domestic violence, for both humans and other animals. This has been the driving force behind all of the projects we have conducted together and that underpin this book.

About Us

I (Nik) am a sociologist who came to research links between human and animal directed violence after years volunteering in animal shelters in the UK. There, I witnessed first-hand the results of the physical and sexual abuse of domestic animals, especially dogs. According to petabuse.com in the US, dogs were the most commonly abused species, accounting for 70.1% of cases, while cats accounted for 20.9% and 'other' animals 24.1% of reported abuse cases in 2011. It was during my time at the animal shelter that I first began to understand the extent of the connection between animal abuse and domestic violence, thanks to a social worker who volunteered at the shelter. At his urging we often fostered the dogs of women entering refuges after fleeing violence, who could not take their animal companions with them, and who refused to leave the violent home until they were assured their animals were safe. This made sense of my early experiences as a teenager in a violent relationship where the perpetrator would often harm his father's dog as a warning to me 'to behave.' At that time, echoing the experiences of many women in violent relationships, I did not know this was a common tactic and so did not know how to speak out about it or who to ask for help.

While I (Nik) have gone on to address human-animal abuse links more broadly in my research (e.g., in slaughterhouses and through meat eating practices), I remain committed to scholar advocacy on behalf of those animals and humans trapped in violent homes because of a general refusal to recognise the importance of other animals and of our relationships with them. This refusal to see, recognise, and work with cross-species relationships means there are few services on offer for humans whose animals are being harmed as part of the violence in their homes. Even fewer are the services on offer for the animals caught in these situations. Few services have allowed animals and their humans to stay together and while, fortunately, this is starting to change the generalised underfunding of the domestic violence service provision sector means there are not enough safe places for human and animal victims of domestic violence (also see Chaps. 5 and 6). Drawing attention to the interconnections of human and animal directed domestic violence is one way to (try to) secure more funding and support for those humans and animals in these situations.

In contrast to Nik, I (Heather) came to work in the area of violence and abuse, specifically domestic violence and child abuse, first as a children's advocate in a local women's shelter and then as a youth worker in residential care for 12–18-year-old young people, most of whom had experienced chronic abuse, neglect, and deprivation. For short periods, early in my career, I also worked in residential care for elderly people, and people with hearing impairments. This was through the 1980s and I can think of no time when the bond many of us have with companion animals was recognised through, for example, their living on, or visiting these, premises. Similarly, as a social worker who graduated in 1988, I spent the next 20 years claiming to love animals but paying no attention to them in my professional practice, including community practices where so many companion animals are housed. Like most social workers, I assumed the concept of 'social' only applied to humans.

I (Heather) grew up in Elizabeth, South Australia, among many other working-class families trying to make their way after migrating to Australia. Throughout my childhood, I lived with companion animals that were loved but, looking back, were not always properly cared for. In our house, domestic violence was a problem for all of us, including our cats and dog. Like some children exposed to domestic violence, these animals were not the direct targets of my father's violence. Yet, they still suffered. They still felt the tensions, the explosions, the yelling, and the destruction. After particularly intense episodes, there were the challenges of trusting not just each other but that there would be the space to let our guards down and relax in each other's company. When we did so, the connections felt even stronger, pulling us together in a shared experience of fear and intimidation. Further complicating matters, and common to many domestic violence dynamics for humans and animals, were the many attempts the animals made to placate my father, to soothe him when they (like us) felt a build-up in his anger that he could control with his boss and mates at the pub but not at home.

Seven years ago, when we began our collaboration, we didn't know that our experiences in animal and human shelter work would converge. Nor did we realise that this work would lead us to very similar shared ideologies regarding issues such as abuse, power, speciesism, domination, and oppression (we discuss our shared theoretical positions in detail in Chap. 2). Both our shared theoretical interests, and our differences in approach, have been crucial to the development of all our work, allowing us to stretch each other's thinking in respectful and dialogic ways. Our deep and intellectually curious friendship has enabled us to challenge ourselves and each other, while feeling supported. We identify with Lopez and Gillespie (2016, 1690) when they talk about the "buddy system," which they characterise as something "developed through our close friendship, our care for and about one another, and our ongoing concern about the emotional toll wrought by solitary research about violent systems and their embodied effects."

As Lopez and Gillespie point out, neoliberal conceptions of research stress disembodied objectivity, which is often at odds with the kind of work feminist researchers do, particularly when they/we focus on aspects of gendered and/or speciesist violence (see Fraser and Taylor 2016). In our view, to not care about the group members we research with and/or for is an unethical and therefore untenable position for us to maintain. Rather than strike the pose of the detached, objective, neutral observer, we argue for transparency of values and trustworthiness in the research process. In part, this is why we shared information about our histories and our positions in the previous paragraphs. Most importantly, we support the longstanding feminist injunction towards praxis, that is, the extension of feminist politics beyond theory, beyond method and into the very research relationship itself. For us, this means acknowledging and supporting each other's journey through the research while at the same time using the emotions it stirs analytically. As Lopez and Gillespie (2016, 1694) put it,

> Grief already underwrites much of our research – we research the things we do precisely because we care. While 'reason' and 'objectivity' are privileged

within research, we argue with other feminist scholars, so too should be emotion … Centering the researchers' emotional responses is a mode of politicising the ways in which they reveal insights about the nature and form of the violent processes we study … we are enacting a kind of caring that reaches beyond the realm of friendship and into a radical form of scholarship that takes into account the very lonely work done by academics even as we acknowledge how very relational and interdependent we are.

As scholar activists we undertake all our work with a view to, at its simplest level, making (at least some) lives better. This book and the projects it is based on are no different. Specifically, we hope to contribute to the collective improvement of the lives of victims/survivors of abuse, both human and animal.

Trigger Warnings and Transformative Education

Before proceeding any further, however, we want to acknowledge the sensitivity of the material explored in this book and the dilemmas we have faced deciding which stories to reveal in this book that illustrate domestic violence in action. We acknowledge that some of the material in the book might be difficult to read and think about, particularly first-hand accounts of being violated. We recognise the possibility of readers—especially those who have survived violence—being triggered or activated. Chapters 4, 5, and 6 contain the most extensive and revealing stories about experiencing violence, so these chapters might be treated with more caution than others.

Vicarious or secondary trauma is not a phenomenon to be ignored or dismissed, as domestic violence workers, and social workers more generally, understand (Bride 2007). Some stories break through our defences, sometimes unexpectedly. We know this from our own experiences as activist-scholars, campaigning against human and animal rights violations. There are times that such exposure is too overwhelming, while at other times, it can feel more manageable. We must collectively persevere because responding to and preventing domestic violence requires us to face some of the harsh realities others experience, if we are to understand and empathise with their plight. In so doing, we must find ways to protect ourselves while remaining sufficiently open, compassionate, and empathic to those most negatively affected by domestic violence.

Whether on the frontline giving support to victims/survivors of domestic violence or undertaking research with people 'in the field' (as we have done), some defences are required to prevent ourselves from becoming overwhelmed and potentially paralysed, particularly by the frequency, gravity, and unfairness of the violence (also see Bride 2007). It can be a delicate position to get right, for frontline workers, researchers, and anti-abuse campaigners alike. It is not easy to find ways to stimulate useful discussions about domestic violence and motivate action—without being gratuitous in the exploration of violence. We are not interested in reproducing examples of violence to shock and distress readers, even under the guise of scholarly study. Yet, we also do not want to sanitise victims' stories or make them more palatable. We have given much thought to selecting excerpts from participants' transcripts, including consideration of the purpose and/or necessity of including explicit content about violence. Yet, caution must still be shown by each reader.

We are also aware that trigger warnings are not themselves unproblematic. Depending on how they are used, trigger warnings can be used to shut down important discussions. While we appreciate their concerns about trigger warnings, we do not share Lukianoff and Haidt's (2015) contention that they inevitably coddle people and are expressions of vindictive protectiveness. We also appreciate that, in and of themselves, trigger warnings cannot prevent the restimulation of past trauma. Instead, we include such a warning here in case it helps readers prepare themselves for the content of this book, especially Chaps. 4, 5, and 6.

Overview of Projects That Underpin This Book

This book is based on work that we have done throughout our respective 20-year-plus careers, including work done prior to our collaboration, and during our partnership over the last 7 years. There is one project, in particular, from which we draw many of our illustrative examples. It is the *Loving You, Loving Me* project, sketched below and detailed in Chap. 3. Findings from other human-animal relationship projects have also informed this book, including a couple led by our friend and colleague, Damien Riggs. While not all of these studies focused explicitly on domestic violence/abuse, they all addressed questions about the depth of connections many people feel with their companion animals. Below we outline the projects that have informed this book.

Loving You, Loving Me (2016–2018)

In 2016 we designed a project to engage the public in discussions about domestic violence and animal abuse. We wanted it to be eye-catching and accessible, dynamic and engaging. We called it the *Loving You, Loving Me* project to place love, not just abuse, at the centre of our inquiry. In doing so we hoped that we might engage people who ordinarily turn away from discussions of abuse, whether because of discomfort, sadness, or long-held beliefs about the lack of importance such discussions had for their lives. Our main partner, the Northern Domestic Violence Service (NDVS), initially raised an eyebrow at the mention of love, perhaps wondering whether this focus would trivialise their clients' experiences of being violated. We understood this and elaborated our rationale. Focusing on love, particularly the experiences of love their clients felt to and from their animal companions, would help to marginalise perpetrators of abuse—symbolically make them recede from view. Written accounts of human and animal experiences of being brutalised would then be analysed to explain how domestic violence can occur and how victims can get stuck in situations that can quickly spiral out of their control. So, we designed a project with two parts: (1) an art and photographic exhibition of human and animal victims surviving violence together and (2) a qualitative study involving interviews with human victims in their homes, in the presence of their companion animals.

For the *Loving You* project we interviewed nine women who had previously experienced domestic violence. Throughout these interviews we focused on their relationships with their companion animals. At the same time, the service providers involved in the project—NDVS and Relationships Australia, South Australia—solicited artworks from the women. These works included original art pieces made by the women and their children as well as photographs of the women and/or their children with their animals taken by volunteers from the local Mawson Lakes Photography Club. The works were exhibited in various municipalities in the north of South Australia, where the project took place. Following a launch that included the local MP, and various speakers on the issue of domestic violence, the exhibition moved throughout the local area. The rationale behind this project, from the very start, was that visual images of animals, and of animals with their humans, would attract attention and open up new spaces to discuss domestic violence as a topic. It would also highlight the importance of services that allow women and their animals to stay together while leaving violence—at the time of writing, NDVS was the only service in the state that did this.

In Good Company: Women and Animal Companions (2014–2015)

This project involved three focus groups, totalling 25 women aged 18–65, where participants talked about their connections to companion animals and shared photographs, stories, and biographies of them. Two groups were held on a university campus and one in a local community organisation. The groups lasted for an hour and were recorded and transcribed. Although there was so much energy that at the end of each session, participants said they wished they were longer. As we explained in Fraser and Taylor (2017), we needed to do relatively little facilitation of discussion. Even complete strangers in the group came alive when talking about their relationships with animal companions, opening up to each other and still chatting to each other and showing more photographs after the sessions had ended. Several participants then joined our Animals in Society Facebook page, https://www.facebook.com/groups/AnimalsInSociety/, which currently stands at a thousand members.

What Is It About Animals? (2015–2016)

This was an openly framed, online project that collected information from humans about their relationship with animal companions. As with most of our work, it included a visual component, so the animals could be present visually. A very broad invitation was made to people over the age of 16 to post images, video, poems, stories, and other texts to a dedicated website about what their animals meant to them. Curious about what a call would bring, we stated simply that "we want to know how you experience animals you consider important; how you describe and feel about these relationships." With 200,000 views from 28,000 unique visitors, we ended up with a total of 94 image posts, 68 of which also included text—almost all from women.

A feminist animal studies perspective, appreciative and critical of speciesism (see Chaps. 2 and 3 for more on our theoretical position), informed the thematic analysis of data produced in both projects. The major theme that emerged from the women's verbal, written, and photographic contributions was that connections to companion animals profoundly enhanced their health and well-being. Linked to this was a clear sense that these deep connections were reciprocal, that is, animals felt them too. Subthemes included recognition of animals' ability to offer unconditional love and regard, act as 'nurses' and therapists, and offer the women the opportunity to experience love, and themselves, in more expansive and holistic ways.

Relationships Between Lesbian, Gay, Bisexual, and/or Transgender People and Their Animal Companions (2016–Present)

With colleagues Damien Riggs (Flinders University), Catherine Donovan (University of Sunderland), and Tania Signal (CQUniversity), we are conducting a series of projects that investigate relationships between lesbian, gay, bisexual, and/or transgender people and their animals. To date, these projects have included analysis of a pre- and post-workshop questionnaire for domestic violence prevention service providers (Riggs et al. 2016), an online survey that focused on both animal companionship and experiences of violence to humans and animals, and had over 500 respondents from the UK and Australia, (see Taylor et al. 2017; Riggs et al. 2018) and interviews with lesbian, bisexual, and/or transgender women regarding the role of companion animals in their health and well-being. Collectively, this data shows that animals are an important source of emotional strength to those experiencing domestic violence and abuse, particularly when they offer non-judgemental support to those who may be experiencing identity-related abuse; that individuals' concern for their animals' well-being can act as a catalyst for leaving the violent relationship; and that animals are emotionally, as well as physically, affected by domestic violence and abuse.

Note on Terminology

We use the terms 'domestic violence' and 'domestic violence and abuse' interchangeably because we define *domestic violence* as any kind of abuse occurring among those who are or have been familial and/or intimate in domestic settings. As discussed later, previous, current, or hoped for experiences of emotional connection and intimacy are centrally related to the ways violence can infiltrate relationships formerly experienced as loving. We use the term domestic violence to signify physical, sexual, psychological, financial, and/or emotional forms of abuse. We recognise that people can be abused without ever having physical violence done to them and that emotional and psychological abuse may happen with or without accompanying physical and/or sexual violence. We also refer to animals as victims of domestic violence and we use the term with the same breadth, that is, we recognise that animals are harmed physically, sexually, emotionally, and psychologically in violent homes. Similarly, we acknowledge that they may suffer without being direct victims of physical harm themselves—through witnessing violence to their humans or through the fear that violent outbursts directed at others engender in animals, for example.

In this book we see domestic violence in gendered terms. We have concentrated most on heterosexual women victims of domestic violence because they are so numerically overrepresented as victims, and also because they were the clients of our primary partner organisation, the NDVS. This does not mean we do not recognise that men can be abused as can those of any gender in same-sex relationships. Both of us completed our undergraduate and post-graduate work, which focused on abuse, working within feminist theories that foregrounded patriarchy as the explanation for men's violence against women, and to a degree we still think this idea has merit. However, more recently in our joint work we have been working with colleagues focusing on animal abuse and domestic violence in the context of LGBTQI people's lives, and this has caused us to re-evaluate our thinking in this area. Put simply, we believe that domestic violence is an abuse of power that can occur between any two people in an intimate relationship. We acknowledge the statistics in this area that show the victims of domestic violence are primarily women in heterosexual relationships with men, who are the abusers (we take this up in more detail in Chap. 2). When we discuss violence in the context of same-sex attracted and/or LGBTI people's lives, we note this specifically.

We use the terms 'companion animal,' 'animal companion,' and 'other animals' throughout, as well as 'animal.' 'Companion animal' and 'animal companions' are used deliberately as we think the term 'pet' is derogatory and suggests that other animals are here solely for human purposes. Our position is that animals have their own lives and agency and need to be recognised as such. Yet our use of the terms companion animal/animal companions is not unproblematic. Whatever terms we use to describe animals that cohabit with humans, the sad fact remains that many are treated badly. Many are left chained outside and not considered part of the family, euthanised as 'unwanted' in their millions at shelters around the world, and, victim to abuse and oppression that denies their liberty and agency. We recognise that, in some ways, using the term companion animal is euphemistic and threatens to gloss over these issues by indicating all is well, that these animals (if not billions of others) are our equal and treated well. We acknowledge this and urge future research into the ways companion animals are treated, and into alternative language that fully expresses the relationship between us and them. For now, though, with alternate language missing, we think this the lesser of two evils and so continue to use the term.

Our use of the terms victims and survivors cuts across human/animal lines. We recognise that there is more to the humans and companion animals described as victims and/or survivors, that these identities are only part of who they are and what they have experienced. We use the terms victims/survivors for shorthanded, explanatory purposes, not to fix their identities as static and unidimensional. We are all more than the classifications into which we are organised. The notion of survival is invoked because, for many victims of domestic violence, the fact that they have survived the violence perpetrated against them is remarkable—a testimony to their/our strength and perseverance. Recognition is also given to the mounting evidence showing that domestic violence is not incidental to neighbourhood disadvantage, that poverty, unemployment, 'tough neighbourhoods' where residents are expected to 'mind their own business' are correlated to and exacerbate domestic violence (Benson et al. 2003). As shown in the diagram by Beyer et al. (2015), four domains inclusive of a range of possibilities influence the likelihood of domestic violence occurring and the likely responses to it. They are (1) individual; (2) interpersonal and family; (3) neighbourhood and community; and (4) policy, systems, and society (Fig. 1.2).

To this diagram we might add a fifth domain: ecological, natural, and built environment. In it we might consider the emerging data showing that climate change, particularly rising temperatures, is being positively correlated to rising numbers of violence-prone individuals, but also the other effects of climate change, such as internal conflicts if not wars over food, water, land, and fuel (see Plante and Anderson 2017). Rather than position (non-human) animals within this ecological domain (as in the amorphous term, flora and fauna), we see them as intersecting all five domains. This is especially relevant to companion animals whose lives and living conditions are directly shaped by all five domains.

Bearing in mind the contextual factors identified in Fig. 1.2, we similarly recognise that there is also more to perpetrators than the abuse they have committed, or are committing, against those they are close to. They too may have been subjected to violence by others, as children in schools and on the streets, and as adults in violent neighbourhoods and bullying workplaces. Many groups of men are still culturally induced into hyperaggressive forms of masculinity, ridiculed if they transgress emotionally

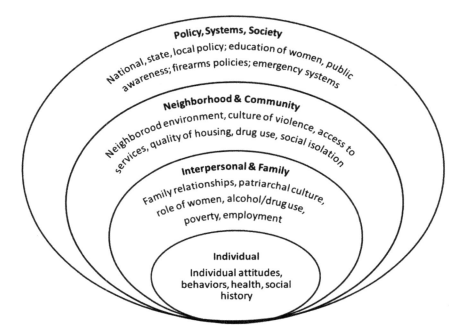

Fig. 1.2 Conceptual model relating individual, social, and ecological factors to intimate partner violence. (Beyer et al. 2015)

repressed, interpersonally dominant codes of conduct so often expected from 'real men.' Some male perpetrators of violence make their living in socially sanctioned violence, such as in abattoirs (Fitzgerald et al. 2009) and through military service and militarism (see, e.g., Adelman 2003). In these work roles, they are to enact violence in very specified ways and disconnect from any moral implications of this violence they might feel. At the same time, they are socially expected to be non-violent in their private lives—a position many fail to maintain (see, e.g., Fitzgerald et al. 2009). We recognise that with the will, support, and resources, perpetrators of abuse can change, and we value the work done to bring about this change. However, this book is not designed to explore the experiences of abusers. If it were, we would have posed research questions that reflected this interest and interviewed them or found other ways to represent their experiences.

Finally, some notes on our use of the term *rescue*. One major theme of the book is rescue, a concept we have deep respect for but also problematise in our considerations of human and companion animal life experiences. Rescue is a notion that at face value suggests something implicitly good, a worthy goal even if not successful. Some rescues are exactly this: ultimately happy stories where victims are plucked from danger into safety, where they are loved and not just allowed to flourish but celebrated for being who they are, whatever that is (dog, cat, female, poor, queer, old, disabled, etc.). However, the idea of rescue is not only something we should exalt.

From a critical perspective, the politics of rescue can involve acts of domination and subordination, often in the name of protection, which is rarely as innocent as it sounds. Think, for instance, about the effects of the Stolen Generation, Sixties Scoop (Sinclair 2007), and other Imperial attempts to 'save' Aboriginal children from their Indigeneity, community connections, and cultures (see Lake 1998). Institutionalised rescue narratives have been used to justify acts of aggression, such as Western attempts to save Iraqi women from the Taliban, and more recently to save homosexuals from other repressive regimes (Bracke 2012). On the face of it these actions seem worthy and commendable. Yet, on closer inspection, the consequences—including those that are unintended—can be dire. First, there is the problem of assuming so many victims possess false consciousness and/or lack self-efficacy, including the ability to take their own actions, including acts of resistance (Bracke 2012). Next is the problem of what happens post-rescue, when rescuers exit often leaving victims to languish in terrible conditions, alone in foreign and/or more hostile situations (see Bracke 2012; Sinclair 2007).

Rescue, in policies and practices with both humans and animals, has had some pernicious consequences. Consider, for instance, the practice of humans rescuing animals without due regard for the long-term consequences and commitments this involves. This includes 'saving' animals only to subject them to further abuse and neglect through animal hoarding (see Berry et al. 2005). Consider all those well-meaning people who orchestrate animal programmes at schools or through petting zoos and the like, who purport to rescue animals but who fail to see when they are being roughly handled, stressed, or, in some instances, disposed of once the programme has ended. In these instances, rescue—as a concept, narrative or practical operation—takes on more sinister meanings.

The social practice of 'rescuing' others has problematic class and gender connotations. Linked, particularly in the case of animal rescue, to female members of the upper classes doing philanthropic work in Victorian Britain, it has often been cast as 'women's work' or as 'emotional work' not relevant to that considered central—and thus lauded—to the (economic) public life of our cultures. In fact, so gendered and misguided were some aspects of animal protectionism considered that the malady of "zoophilpsychosis" (purported 'too much' concern for other animals) was invented to undermine the work of female antivivisectionists in the nineteenth century (Buettinger 1993). This lives on with animal rescue being considered the domain of 'crazy cat ladies' (Fraser and Taylor 2018), and linked to this is the problematic 'saviour complex' that positions humans who work towards improving other animals' lives as being voices for the voiceless (we discuss this in more detail in Chap. 7). Both of these are linguistic moves that simultaneously derogate both the humans and animals involved by reminding us that they are both (often) considered second-class citizens. Our criticisms of this are not intended to occlude the fact that animal rescue (and aligned animal protection movements) is largely the domain and work of women (Coulter and Fitzgerald 2018; Gaarder 2011) but to point out that because of the intersections of misogyny and speciesism this is often assumed to be a bad thing.

Chapter Outlines

In Chap. 2 ('The Links In-and-Between Human-Animal Abuses: Love, Loyalty, and Pain') the links between human and animal abuses are examined, particularly domestic violence. It is here that we explain our use of intersectionality as a theoretical means for understanding interlocking privilege and oppression, as they apply to humans but also (other) animals. We then outline our central argument—that other animals need to be considered in our understandings of domestic violence despite this necessitating a change to the current humancentric thinking and theorising.

In Chap. 3 ('What We Choose to Hear: Researching Human-Animal Violence') we provide a detailed discussion of the methodological approach we took to our projects and to our research more generally into domestic violence and abuse. Research quandaries related to trying to include, or at least see, animals in studies about human-animal relations are then discussed, with illustrative examples provided from our projects such as *What Is It About Animals?* (2016) and *Loving You, Loving Me: Companion Animals and Domestic Violence* (2017).

In Chap. 4 ('Being Subjected to Domestic Violence: Empathic Love and Domination') we consider how women and companion animals are dominated and abused by 'loved ones' and how they seek refuge in each other through their own interspecies relationships of empathic love. Close-up examples of abuse are provided from the *Loving You, Loving Me* study used to consider what it means to construct companion animals as family members in the context of domestic violence. This means it is not just the benefits of 'pet-keeping' for humans that we consider, but the harms caused to all victims of domestic violence, human, and animal. The chapter is broadly organised in terms of chronology and the plot of escaping domestic violence, showing how confusing and complicated it can be when abuse surfaces not as a single incident but an ongoing dynamic. We move through the experiences of love relationships that become abusive, forcing victims to re-evaluate their ongoing viability. The chapter closes with stories about the women deliberating about leaving violent family homes and the likely implications for companion animals in the process.

In Chap. 5 ('Foregrounding Companion Animals' Experiences of Domestic Violence') we consider the impact of domestic violence on animals' physical and mental health and well-being. Because we are equally concerned about animal and human victims/survivors of domestic violence, this means that just as we pay attention to the impact of domestic violence on humans we also have to pay attention to the impact on companion animals. Similarly, as we consider how humans embark on their recovery after leaving domestic violence, along with their animal companions, so too we need to address the animals' recovery.

In Chap. 6 ('Supporting Victims/Survivors: Escape, Refuge, and Recovery') the themes are escape, refuge, and recovery. These are used to analyse how victims/survivors managed to escape domestic violence in their homes and how they (try to) recover from the violence and rebuild their lives with the support of others. Participants stressed the importance of housing, so we pay attention to their attempts to find alternative housing that would accommodate themselves and their children, but also their animal companions. We present other challenges to recovering from violence by 'loved ones' to show that in contrast to the popular fantasy of escape, post-separation may not be experienced as liberating but as another period of anxiety and hardship.

In the concluding chapter ('The Work of Significant Other/s: Companion Animal Relationships in the Future') we reflect on historical changes associated with feminists making domestic violence a public not just personal problem. Our interest in the love, empathy, and healing possibilities of human-animal companionship continues in this chapter through our discussion of the need to value the labour that companion animals perform, especially their emotion work. We argue that recognising their labour necessitates us thinking about what companion animals might get out of their relationships with humans and whether they are 'voiceless.' We note the need to also think in practical terms about the necessary provisions for animals in the context of domestic violence, including suitable housing for human and animal victims. For illustrative and inspirational purposes, we point to several current relevant policy and programme examples. We end with a discussion of six key commitments that need to be shown by humans towards companion animals for the notion of significant other to become truly meaningful.

References

Adelman, M. (2003). The military, militarism, and the militarization of domestic violence. *Violence Against Women, 9*(9), 1118–1152.

AIHW. (2018). *Family, domestic and sexual violence in Australia, 2018*. Retrieved July 23, 2018, from https://www.aihw.gov.au/reports/domestic-violence/family-domestic-sexual-violence-in-australia-2018/contents/summary

Benson, M. L., Fox, G. L., DeMaris, A., & Van Wyk, J. (2003). Neighborhood disadvantage, individual economic distress and violence against women in intimate relationships. *Journal of Quantitative Criminology, 19*(3), 207–235.

Berry, C., Patronek, G., & Lockwood, R. (2005). Long-term outcomes in animal hoarding cases. *Animal Law, 11*, 167–193.

Beyer, K., Wallis, A. B., & Hamberger, L. K. (2015). Neighborhood environment and intimate partner violence: A systematic review. *Trauma, Violence & Abuse, 16*(1), 16–47.

Bracke, S. (2012). From 'saving women' to 'saving gays': Rescue narratives and their dis/continuities. *European Journal of Women's Studies, 19*(2), 237–252.

Bride, B. E. (2007). Prevalence of secondary traumatic stress among social workers. *Social Work, 52*(1), 63–70.

Buettinger, C. (1993). Antivivisection and the charge of zoophil-psychosis in the early twentieth century. *The Historian, 55*(2), 277–232.

Coulter, K., & Fitzgerald, A. (2018). The compounding feminization of animal cruelty investigation work and its multispecies implications. *Gender, Work and Organization*, online first, http://onlinelibrary.wiley.com/doi/10.1111/gwao.12230/full

Fitzgerald, A. J., Kalof, L., & Dietz, T. (2009). Slaughterhouses and increased crime rates: An empirical analysis of the spillover from "The Jungle" into the surrounding community. *Organization & Environment, 22*(2), 158–184.

Fraser, H., & Taylor, N. (2016). *Neoliberalization, universities and the public intellectual: Species, gender and class in the production of knowledge*. London: Palgrave.

Fraser, H., & Taylor, N. (2017). In good company: Women, companion animals, and social work. *Society & Animals, 25*(4), 341–361.

Fraser, H., & Taylor, N. (2018). *Women, anxiety, and companion animals: Toward a feminist animal studies of interspecies care and solidarity*. London/New York: Bloomberg.

Gaarder, E. (2011). *Women and the animal rights movement*. New York: Rutgers University Press.

Garcia-Moreno, C., & Watts, C. (2011). Violence against women: An urgent public health priority. *Bulletin of the World Health Organization, 89*, 2–2.

García-Moreno, C., Jansen, H. A., Ellsberg, M., Heise, L., & Watts, C. (2005). *WHO multi-country study on women's health and domestic violence against women: Initial results on prevalence, health outcomes and women's responses*. Geneva: World Health Organization.

Lake, M. (1998). Feminism and the gendered politics of antiracism, Australia 1927–1957: From maternal protectionism to leftist assimilationism. *Australian Historical Studies, 29*(110), 91–108.

Lopez, P., & Gillespie, K. (2016). A love story: For "buddy system research" in the academy. *Gender, Place and Culture, 23*(12), 1689–1700.

Lukianoff, G., & Haidt, J. (2015). The coddling of the American mind. *The Atlantic, 316*(2), 42–52.

NCADV. (2018). *National Coalition Against Domestic Violence.* Retrieved July 23, 2018, from https://ncadv.org/statistics

Patronek, G. J. (1997). Issues for veterinarians in recognizing and reporting animal neglect and abuse. *Society & Animals, 5*(3), 267–280.

Petabuse.com. *Animal cruelty statistics.* Retrieved July 23, 2018, from http://www.humanesociety.org/issues/abuse_neglect/facts/animal_cruelty_facts_statistics.html?referrer=https://www.google.com.au/#victims

Pizzey, E. (1974). *Scream quietly or the neighbours will hear.* Harmondsworth: Penguin Books.

Plante, C., & Anderson, C. A. (2017). Global warming and violent behavior. *APS Observer, 30*(2), 29–32.

Riggs, D. W., Fraser, H., Taylor, N., Signal, T., & Donovan, C. (2016). Domestic violence service providers' capacity for supporting transgender women: Findings from an Australian workshop. *British Journal of Social Work, 46*, 2374–2392.

Riggs, D. W., Taylor, N., Signal, T., Fraser, H., & Donovan, C. (2018). People of diverse genders and/or sexualities and their animal companions: Experience of family violence in a bi-national sample. *Journal of Family Issues*, online first, https://doi.org/10.1177/0886260518771681

Sinclair, R. (2007). Identity lost and found: Lessons from the sixties scoop. *First Peoples Child & Family Review, 3*(1), 65–82.

Statistics Canada. (2016). *Family violence in Canada: A statistical profile.* Retrieved July 23, 2018, from https://www150.statcan.gc.ca/n1/pub/85-002-x/2018001/article/54893-eng.htm

Taylor, N., Fraser, H., & Riggs, D. W. (2017). Domestic violence and companion animals in the context of LGBT people's relationships. *Sexualities*, online first, https://doi.org/10.1177/1363460716681476

Fig. 2.1 Woman with terrier on knee

2

The Links In-and-Between Human-Animal Abuses: Love, Loyalty, and Pain

Introduction

This chapter starts with an overview of the current literature documenting the links between human and animal abuses and is focused on the abuse of humans and companion animals in private homes. The reported and likely effects on victims/survivors are then identified, for humans and companion animals. We argue that current mainstream frameworks for understanding domestic violence are inadequate and that this is especially evident when we try to extend them to an understanding of domestic violence done to other animals. Instead, we argue that a more expansive understanding of domestic violence is required; one that draws on feminist intersectional Understandings of power that allows us to include animals in their own right. An added advantage of this is it allows an exploration of how love and abuse can coexist in domestic settings for humans and animals which we consider in the second section of this chapter. The themes of love, loyalty, and pain provide context and insights into the complexities, shock, and confusion so many humans and companion animals feel being subjected to domestic violence. As shown, in much of

© The Author(s) 2019
N. Taylor, H. Fraser, *Companion Animals and Domestic Violence*, Palgrave Studies in Animals and Social Problems, https://doi.org/10.1007/978-3-030-04125-0_2

the human-animal literature these themes of love, loyalty, and pain appear through discussions of (human) victims delaying leaving because of concerns about housing and the safety of their companion animals.

Our main conceptual argument is then clarified. Simply put it is that we need to extend the current framing of domestic violence to include animals as victims in their own right. This shift in conceptualisation is intended to help us move away from a humancentric approach to understanding domestic violence, one that includes their direct experiences of abuse but also them witnessing the abuse of their humans.

Framing Domestic Violence and Ascertaining Its Impact

Studies about domestic violence have mushroomed since the 1970s. As a result, many statistics can be cited to show prevalence, incidence, severity, and costs to individuals, particular populations, wider societies, and so on. In a time where we have seen the rise of (narrowly defined) evidence-based practice, readers might implore us to 'show us the numbers.' In part, we have responded to this call citing dozens of studies from around the world. However, we need to remember that different definitions of domestic violence are used in studies that deploy a wide variety of methods, applied in a range of contexts, all of which make clean comparisons of data difficult, if not impossible, particularly in relation to questions about prevalence and incidence. Our appreciation of these complexities means that rather than assume that the findings we will cite in this book are context-less and universally generalisable, we refer to a host of studies—recent and older—to pick up the threads of commonality and point to common patterns of knowledge.

For instance, in countries such as Australia, we know that domestic violence is a widespread, serious social problem. According to the Australian Bureau of Statistics (2013), one in three women has experienced physical and/or sexual violence perpetrated by someone known to them and one in four women (and one in seven men) has experienced emotional abuse by a partner (ABS 2014). These figures are similar to those in comparable countries, for example, in Canada in 2015 almost 92,000 were victims of intimate partner violence as reported to the police. Four out of five of these were women (79%)—representing about 72,000 female victims (Burczycka and Conroy 2017). In the European Union (EU), interviews with 42,000 women across the 28 member states of the EU (EUFRA 2015) demonstrated that an estimated 13 million women in the EU had experienced physical violence and 3.7 million women had experienced sexual assault in the 12 months before the interviews, that one in three women (33%) had experienced physical and/or sexual violence since she was 15 years old with 8% of women having experienced physical and/or sexual violence in the 12 months before the interviews. And in the US, more than one in three women (35.6%) have experienced rape, physical violence, and/or stalking by an intimate partner in their lifetime; nearly one in ten women (9.4%) has been raped by an intimate partner in her lifetime, and around one in four women (24.3%) have experienced severe physical violence by an intimate partner (Black et al. 2011).

Less is known about the prevalence of violence done to companion animals within domestically violent relationships because of a lack of data due in part to poor responses from a criminal justice system that does not take animal abuse as seriously as human abuse. This is compounded by the fact that the human services that may encounter animal abuse (such as domestic violence shelters) tend not to keep systematic records of it (if they keep records about animals at all), and by the fact that the investigation of cruelty to animals is often done by underfunded SPCAs (Societies for the Prevention of Cruelty to Animals) that do not have the resources to fully prosecute all perpetrators. For instance, the Royal Society for the Prevention of Cruelty to Animals (RSPCA 2013) estimates that only 3% of prosecutions result in convictions due to a lack of prosecutable evidence. To put this in context, the operational statistics annual report of the RSPCA in England and Wales shows that of the 1,327,849 calls to a 24-hour cruelty line, 153,770 allegations of cruelty were investigated, with 2174 cases being reported to the RSPCA prosecutions department. While few of these complaints will be regarding deliberate companion animal abuse, it demonstrates the problems inherent in using official sources to assess the prevalence of companion animal abuse as many cases of animal abuse reported to the SPCA (or equivalent body) never make it to the official statistics. Attempts to quantify the prevalence of animal abuse outside of the official statistics are also problematic. For example, while data demonstrates that around 40% of veterinarians see between one and three cases of deliberate abuse per year (in Australia; Green and Gullone 2005), many animal victims of deliberate abuse will not be taken to the vet (Arluke and Irvine 2017). Tiplady et al. (2012) interviewed 26 women with experiences of domestic violence and found only 2 of them (8%) reported specifically mentioning animal abuse to the veterinarian treating their animal despite a number of animals reportedly being euthanised due to injuries suffered. The remaining 24 women (92%) explained that they would be hesitant about discussing animal abuse with a veterinarian due to (1) general shame regarding the abuse, (2) a fear of being judged or a fear the veterinarian would not believe them, and (3) a fear of the consequences if the abuser found out they had spoken to a veterinarian.

Despite this general lack of evidence regarding deliberate animal abuse, studies have repeatedly demonstrated links between domestic violence and animal abuse, including child and elder abuse. In particular, there is ample evidence of higher rates of threatened and actual harm of animals in relationships where domestic violence (towards humans) is occurring (e.g., Ascione et al. 1997; Volant et al. 2008). Volant et al. (2008), for example, compared the experiences of 102 Australian women who had experienced domestic violence and abuse with a demographically matched sample of 102 women without similar experience. They found that more than half the women who had experienced domestic violence and abuse reported their animal companions had been harmed, and 17% of these reported that their animal companions had been killed. This contrasted with only 6% of the matched sample reporting harm of animals, and no animal companion deaths. This matches international research that demonstrates co-occurrence of domestic violence and animal abuse rates between 25% and 86% (Monsalve et al. 2017). For example, Hartman et al. (2016), in a US study, found that 11.7% of 291 victims of domestic violence had witnessed threats towards a companion animal, with 26.1% witnessing actual animal harm. The presence of animal abuse in families where other forms of domestic violence are occurring has been linked to more severe and more forms of violence towards humans, along with a greater use of controlling behaviours. Simmons and Lehmann (2007) in their survey of 1283 women seeking refuge in domestic violence shelters in Texas, between 1998 and 2002, found that men who abuse the family companion animal appear to be more dangerous than men who do not. The animal-abusing men demonstrated more instances of sexual violence, marital rape, emotional violence, and stalking than men who did not abuse the family companion animal. They also used a wider variety of controlling behaviours.

Human abusers can deliberately target companion animals to maintain the human victim's compliance, silence, or to punish perceived wrongs committed (e.g., DeGue and DiLillo 2009). In a study in Ireland, Allen et al. (2006) asked 13 women (of a sample of 23) who had experienced animal abuse in their domestically violent relationship, what they thought motivated the abuser's behaviour. Of these women, 12 believed their animals were used to deliberately establish control over them and/or their children. Even when they gave other reasons, such as anger and revenge, the majority of the women read this back to being another form of control. Similarly, Newberry (2017), in her analysis of 74 stories from online forums where individuals shared experiences of companion animal abuse, found that using animals to control human behaviour was a common theme. Within this theme she identified three subthemes: isolating victims by restricting their contact with others (e.g., victims scared to leave their animals with the perpetrator while they visited friends/family), financial control (e.g., refusal to pay for veterinary fees), and preventing victims from leaving and/or coercing them to come back (e.g., threatening animals' lives if victims were to leave).

Questions About Victims Leaving

Concern for the well-being of their animals (or 'fellow sufferers') (Fitzgerald 2007) often results in those who experience domestic violence delaying leaving, remaining in, or returning to abusive relationships (e.g., Ascione et al. 2007; Faver and Strand 2003; Newberry 2017). Allen et al. (2006) document how 4 of the 13 women in their study had delayed leaving because of concerns over their animals' well-being. This was compounded by children's attachments to companion animals. Allen et al.'s respondents explicitly mentioned that lack of domestic violence services that include companion animals was a significant factor in their decision to remain in the violent relationship. This mirrors other research that shows between 18% and 65% of female victims of domestic violence delay leaving over concern for their animals' well-being (Monsalve et al. 2017). Service providers are increasingly articulating that concern for the well-being of any animals left behind is a significant barrier to leaving violent situations (e.g., Wuerch et al. 2017). Concern over companion animal's well-being is also a factor that makes some women return to violent relationships. Carlisle-Frank et al. (2004) surveyed 48 women who had experience of domestic violence, 34 of whom had companion animals. They found that of those who had companion animals, 48% had considered returning to the violent home due to concerns for their animals, 25% had at some point actually returned to the abuser out of concern for their companion animals, and 35% had returned to the abuser out of concern for their animals in cases where the batterer had previously abused the pet.

Long-Term Effects of Domestic Violence

Extensive research across disciplinary boundaries shows the long-term and devastating effects for the many who experience domestic violence. Well documented are the short- and long-term psychological problems for all human victims/survivors and, for children, increased risk of behavioural and educational problems (Geffner et al. 2003). Mental and physical health problems, including post-traumatic distress, anxiety, depression, are common, as is substance use as a form of self-medication (Zlotnick et al. 2006). Homelessness and a loss of economic stability and security are also outcomes of experiencing domestic violence for many women (Mayock et al. 2016). Increasingly research is also documenting the ill effects of witnessing animal abuse within domestically violent homes, particularly for children. Research demonstrates that children living in homes where domestic violence is present also witness more cruelty to animals than in homes without domestic violence (Volant et al. 2008). Children exposed to domestic violence are at increased risk of behavioural, socio-emotional, and cognitive difficulties (Øverlien 2010) and, in the case of witnessing co-occurring animal abuse and domestic violence, appear to be at higher risk of harming other animals. For example, Ascione (1998) reported that 32% of the 22 women with children who sought shelter at a safe house he interviewed stated that a child had hurt or killed a family pet. Similarly, comparing a sample of 47 mothers and 94 children (between the ages of 5 and 17) who had a history of domestic violence and a comparison group with no domestic violence history, Currie (2006) found that children in the exposed group were 2.95 times more likely to engage in animal cruelty than children in the non-exposed group.

Children may also be at increased risk of harm directed to them through their connections with their companion animals. McDonald et al. (2015) interviewed 58 children who had experienced threats to harm their animals or had heard or seen someone harm or kill their animals. McDonald et al. report that children often utilised preventative strategies to stop their mothers' partners harming companion animals. For example, they would hide the animals in their rooms or take them outside. Some would directly confront the abuser in order to prevent them harming their animals. As well as increasing the risk for the children this, McDonald et al. note, affects the mothers by exacerbating the "negative psychological and emotional consequences of living with IPV [interpersonal violence] and lead to feelings of guilt, self-blame and reduced confidence in their role as a mother" (123).

It is clear, then, that there are links between domestic violence and animal abuse: where one is present, the other is highly likely. There are also links between the forms that this violence and abuse takes as well as responses across the (human and other animal) species to it. Accordingly, finding a way to conceptualise and respond to domestic violence that is inclusive of all species' experiences is important. As we detail later in this chapter, feminist intersectional theories that understand domestic violence as a mechanism of power are particularly useful for this. They are useful precisely because they acknowledge the centrality of power and allow us to see similarities in the mechanisms used and structures that support the use of violence. Also important is recognising the connections between love and abuse. Love is relevant to domestic violence because, ironically, love relationships can open the door to domination, coercion, and control.

Recognising the Links Between Love, Abuse, and Loyalty

The love relationships relevant to this book are varied. Among humans, they may—or may not—involve romantic ideation; sexual intimacy; friendship and companionship; strong bonds of emotional attachment; a sense of belonging, security, safety; equality, respect, and participation in decision-making; and freedom of expression, including the right to be different—all of which has relevance to *affective equality*, a concept calling for democracy in intimate relations (see Lynch et al. 2016). Between humans and (other) animals, these relationships can be founded on love, affection, play, respect, and/or loyal servitude, often exemplified by the concept of dogs staying true to their 'masters.' Crucially, the love relationships most publicly sanctioned and cherished for women are likely to involve humans, specifically heterosexual male partners.

Despite this, many people testify to the strong bonds of love felt for, and between, other species. For example, Charles (2017, 122) in her investigation of intimacy and kinship in human-(companion) animal relations notes that "What is striking about the written accounts [of shared lives] is the intensity of the emotions that are represented and the way that correspondents write their life stories through their accounts of the animals with whom they have been involved since childhood." Charles notes that when people write anonymously about their relations with other animals, and thus have no, or less, fear of moral censure, the emotional intensity of their experiences become apparent. People, for instance, liken their relationships to 'falling in love' and often focus on 'enchantment' or "the power to enchant and to move her [respondent] to love" (p. 124).

The Contradictions of Love

However, we should not be fooled into thinking that love is as innocent as it first sounds. Because so much abuse is perpetrated in the name of love, it is worth spending time exploring their interconnections (also see Fraser 2008). What do we mean when we speak of 'love?' And for women and companion animals, who are the focus of this book, what are the links between love, abuse, and loyalty?

Simple definitions of complex phenomenon such as love are tempting but misleading. If there is a single truth about love, it is that it has multiple meanings, applications, and referents (Oord 2005) making it hard to define and capture. Love can be a noun, an adjective, and a verb, and can refer to any number of experiences. For instance, love is sometimes declared for inanimate objects (or commodities), such as cars, houses, boats, and shoes. People report loving particular games such as football or tennis or processes such as meditating or cooking. For some, their love of and for the land is the cornerstone of their spiritual identities and sense of belonging, as it is for many Indigenous and First Nations peoples (see Rigsby 1999). For many companion animals, love is expressed towards family members that they trust and enjoy being in their company. They may also 'love' objects such as toys, balls, or bedding but also interactions, such as games and outings, especially those where they are able to engage in free play in natural environments.

Whether produced in research or popular culture, definitions of love inevitably speak to values, beliefs, and theoretical inclinations. Most focus exclusively on human-human love relations. Some present accounts where the psychology of love is all-important. In these accounts, love may be conceptualised as an affective state, a basic emotion (Shaver et al. 1996) and a moral emotion (Velleman 1999). Through this lens, love as a moral emotion helps to differentiate it from narcissism (see Campbell et al. 2002), co-dependence, and sex addiction (Carnes 2013), which mainstream psychology classify as pathologies. In pop-psychology, this is translated to mean avoiding others defined as either 'commitment phobes' (those averse to committing to long-term monogamy) or, conversely, those classified as 'anxiously attached,' which in popular social media vernacular may be called 'stage 5 clingers.'

From some socio-cultural and linguistic perspectives, love is variously conceptualised as a discourse (Wetherell 1995), a narrative (Wood 2001), or a story (Sternberg 1995). From this collection of perspectives there is an interest in the politics associated with loving others, for instance, the often-substantial emotional work performed in its name (see, e.g., Wood 2001). It is the work reported to maintain love relationships, especially romantic, sexualised love, motivated by the assumption that it is through these relationships that the deepest and most lasting bonds can be made possible (see Noller 1996). For others, especially second-wave feminists, ever-after-love is more accurately understood as a utopian fantasy or illusion (see Illouz 1997)—a gendered injunction towards romantic love, and a cultural imperative, especially for women (see Benjamin 2013; Illouz 1997; Wood 2001). Feminists have an extensive history teaching us that romantic love is especially problematic, particularly for heterosexual women (Benjamin 2013; Kearney 2001; Radway [1984] 2009), but also for other groups marginalised in the process, across genders, sexualities, and other identities of difference, including species. Black feminists and those inclined towards post-colonial theory have rightly pointed out how we can be othered by love, objectified by loved ones as exotic. Scholarly debates continue in relation to whether love is best seen as an art (see Fromm 2000) or a science (see Walsh 1991). From a scientific, evolutionary perspective, love is a biologically driven imperative to reproduce and survive (see, e.g., Fisher et al. 2006; Fletcher et al. 2015). From this view, romance is a chimera (illusion) used for the purposes of reproduction and survival. From a scientific perspective, Oord (2005, 923) asks,

> Is love a decision or a feeling? blind or universally aware? sexual, nonsexual, or asexual? self-sacrificial or self-authenticating? unconditional or object-specific? Is love best understood as agape, eros, philia, something else, or all of these and more?

Oord (2005) asked these questions in an attempt to scientifically quantify love, defining love simply as sympathetic intentions and behaviours shown by individuals towards loved ones. In our feminist intersectional view, attempts to scientifically capture love through measurement are well-meaning but invariably reductionist, as they rely on the use of narrow preordained definitions of love into which observed, reported, perceived, and remembered experiences of love are squeezed. Erased are culture, politics, and the materialities of love relationships—all of which influence their nature, shape, and viability. Erased too, for the most part, is the idea of a non-pathologised love that can be felt across species (note, we do not mean bestiality or sex with other animals here, but emotional ties). The contexts for love relationship matter, and the exclusive focus on individuals, psychology, and pathology is reductionist, along with the dichotomies many professionals use to distinguish real love from infatuation, mature love from immature love, and functional love from the dysfunctional love kind (see Noller 1996). From our perspective, love is best understood in multiple terms affecting all of life's domains (materiality, psychology, sociality, physiology, emotionality, and spirituality), across structural divisions of humans (through gender, class, race, etc.) and across the human/animal divide. The challenge for us studying love in relation to domestic violence is to appreciate its theoretical complexities while still maintaining a moral and ethical stance against violence. Part of our research process has been to recognise the contradictions of love experienced by our research participants (see Chaps. 4, 5, and 6).

The history of love and associated expressions of love, such as loyalty, have long been considered not just for the power of love to deliver benefits, but also the potential costs, restrictions, and pain associated with loving others, (Frieze 2005). Interpersonally, we know there are many contradictions associated with loving others: "We say that love hurts, love waits, love stinks, and love means never having to say you're sorry" (Oord 2005, 922). Many people appreciate the contradictions of people hurting the ones they (say they) love (Frieze 2005), intuitively if not consciously. This is evident through colloquialisms such as 'love and abuse are different sides of the same coin.'

Around the world, stories of love are told in great abundance but not all love stories are treated with the same recognition and regard. Social media, in particular, is saturated with references to love, especially interspecies connections. Yet, it is monogamous heterosexual coupledom that usually dominates mainstream contemporary Western societies about what it means to find *real/true love*.

For oppressed groups, such as women and companion animals, love relationships are popularly represented and often sought out because they offer opportunities to be recognised as worthy of love, individual recognition, and a place to call home. Not so well covered are the dangers of love and loyalty facing women and companion animals, especially for those with past histories of abuse. Of the many current realities faced in the field of domestic violence is the fact that prior experiences of domestic violation elevate, rather than decrease, future risks of being violated in a domestic setting. From the research we know that this applies to humans (see, e.g., Milaniak and Widom 2015). We do not know if this also applies to companion animals too. In other words, the cruel twist is that abuse experienced in childhood (or puppyhood, kittenhood) makes further abuse in adulthood more likely not less.

To recap, love is relevant to domestic violence because it is often through love relationships that domination, coercion, and control take place, often under the guise of romance and passion (see Benjamin 2013; Frieze 2005; Kearney 2001). Merging with another through love can be a risky business. More than a century ago, E.A. Singer (1916) raised questions about the tensions between loving others as a way for humans to individuate (e.g., being recognised as a unique individual) and being tied to loved ones from a sense of loyalty. He asked,

> Is love the only thing that individuates? (Singer 1916, 460).... it has generally been supposed that love was less the art of individuating and more the art of yielding. But this is just the mistake that has prevented love from taking its place among the more seriously meant categories of philosophy and the realities of life; for this yielding disposition that might be supposed to make for peace in a republic of lovers is the very matter which introduces trouble and perplexity there. (Singer 1916, 462)

For us, questions about individuating and yielding in love relationships help us to understand the potential for love and abuse to coexist—how abuse can exploit lovers' sense of loyalty and hopes for the future. There is extensive literature illustrating how dominating 'the bonds of love' can be (Benjamin 2013). We are especially interested in love relationships that are, have been, or hold the promise of becoming a family, as this hope or aspiration can help hold women and companion animals as hostage in domestic violence situations, either temporarily or over long periods of time.

Earlier we explained how abuse by (former) loved ones usually punctures human and animal victims' sense of trust and belonging, and can confound their understanding of what, if anything, this means for their relationships. Violence by a loved one can be a shocking betrayal that many understandably find hard to process and accept as an ongoing reality (Wood 2001), name as abuse (Fraser 2008), and reach out for help (Campo and Tayton 2015). For non-abusive others, seeking help for others in the family who have been victimised can be a frightening endeavour, such as an abused woman taking an abused child to a doctor, or an abused cat to a vet. Negative judgements abound about those who 'remain with perpetrators' (see Fraser 2005), a perverse irony, given it can be so difficult to relocate to new and safer domestic settings with companion animals, and that it is during this period of separation that is the most dangerous, for human and animal victims—certainly the time when the most fatalities occur. To quote Mouzos and Rushforth (2003, 2), "women who have separated are at higher risk of homicide victimisation by intimate partners than women in current relationships."

Often, part of the confusing deliberation process for victims after an episode of domestic violence includes grappling with the cultural and often gendered, ageist, and speciesist injunctions about loyalty—that female intimates, young people, and companion animals should show loyalty—no matter what. Women, children, and dogs are the most obvious targets of this cultural injunction that they should remain steadfastly loyal to others in the face of hardship and adversity, which, in the case of domestic violence, can mean not disclosing abuse to others, actively concealing the abuse for fear of retribution, and/or internalising responsibility for the abuse. For Indigenous women involved in love relationships with other Indigenous people, the ties of loyalty through the shared experience of colonisation and associated police brutality further complicate the possibility of disclosing abuse when it is happening (Campo and Tayton 2015). For non-Indigenous victims of domestic violence perpetrated by Indigenous partners, the bonds of love and ties of loyalty may also shape non-Indigenous victims' appreciation of how colonisation, in the past and today, and its influence on policing and other state authorities act as barriers in naming (racialised) perpetrators of violence.

For members of oppressed groups (devalued through, e.g., sexism, ageism, and speciesism), violence at home often places victims in invidious positions, where they will usually have to face some unenviable future possibilities. There are structural and material considerations, not just those pertaining to psychology and culture (Wood 2001). For groups susceptible to economic poverty and resource scarcity (such as women, children, and animals), love relationships with higher status others offer opportunities to shore up a better future (through, e.g., a place to live and a food source), not just a potential escape from loneliness and social isolation. By extension, the termination of these relationships can threaten more than emotional states, but health and well-being, including for some, such as 'pets' abandoned or surrendered, their immediate survival. As participants in our *Loving You, Loving Me* study showed, victims' fears of leaving abusive partners and problems accessing decent alternative housing are warranted, specifically women with companion animals.

Acknowledging that love and abuse coexist is an important step in moving away from romanticised versions of (heterosexual, romantic) love. We need to recognise that strong bonds of affection and love can exist between and across species divides. Both of these are important if we are to find ways to better help women and animals suffering from domestic violence. Understanding that ties may exist that prevent women from leaving violent relationships, or that contribute to their decisions to return, needs to be woven into any discussions of the development of services to assist them to leave abuse with their animal companions. Key to this is changing the way we think about domestic violence in terms of its definition and its ability to capture the experience of non-human animals.

Our Position

There are multiple theories regarding domestic violence. Broadly speaking they can be broken into two main approaches: structural and individual. Individualised approaches see violence within the family as the consequence of individual pathology. Structural approaches differ in that they focus on how violence is an outcome of social systems (Lawson 2012) which leads to a focus on social inequality, primarily the inequality between genders (although not limited to this as class, income, ethnicity, and dis/ability all play a part in domestic violence and our responses to it, see the later discussion on intersectionality). Feminist approaches are structural in that their primary focus, or unit of analysis, is the power differences between men and women. As Yllö points out (2005, 19): "Domestic violence cannot be adequately understood unless gender and power are taken into account."

Following feminist accounts and influenced by service provider perspectives that are based on listening to women survivors, we take domestic violence to be a range of coercive behaviours (physical, sexual, emotional, financial) that aim to control through intimidation, threats, or actual harm. Most endemic is domestic violence in heterosexual relationships where men try to control women.[1] More broadly, we see this as a function of asymmetrical power in relationships that is held by the individual (men, in our studies) but is backed up by various cultural tropes embedded in institutional practices and discourses such as those about romantic love and the property status of other animals. Domestic violence, then, in this book is considered to be a "deeply embedded political-economic-cultural phenomena with wider social formations" (Hearn 2012, 160) that is the outcome of various embedded practices that reflect gender imbalances and male domination at a societal level.

At the same time the definition used throughout this book acknowledges intersectionality (Crenshaw 1991): that the structures and systems that create and maintain discrimination and oppression (in this case domestic violence) occur across other socially overvalued and devalued identity categories associated with sexuality, race, class, ability, age, religion, and geographical location. While discrimination and oppression manifest at a micro level (in the home, in the case of domestic violence), they are inextricably linked to macro processes and structures. This intersectional analysis of domestic violence as coercion allows the inclusion of other species for they are also victims of coercion in the family dynamic. It is precisely their status as *animal*, as less-than-human and as commodity and property that facilitates the violence done to them, as well as explains the relative lack of services for them (and the humans they live with) (Fraser et al. 2017). In short, our contention is that intersectional

---

[1] For accounts of violence in same-sex relationships, see Donovan and Hester 2014, Kelly 1996. For debates on the a/symmetry of violence done to men and women, see Kelly and Westmarland 2016, Lawson 2012.

analyses—extended to include other species—allow us to take seriously the abuse of other animals and respond to the violence and neglect they experience.

In popular discourse this acknowledgement of interlinked human-animal abuse is often framed in terms of 'The Link.' 'The Link' is a reference to the various interconnections between human and animal abuse, not simply to those found in domestic violence. In mainstream discourse, 'The Link' has increasingly become a consideration of whether animal abuse is a signal for later or concurrent human-directed abuse (Ascione 1998). As a result, a great deal of time and effort has gone into investigating whether a causal link between human- and animal-directed violence exists, and what its contours may look like. This has led to a preponderance of work assessing the diagnostic utility of human-animal abuse theses. While such diagnostic approaches have pragmatic utility, they remain mired in conceptual approaches and theoretical frameworks that posit human interests as more important than those of other species (Taylor and Signal 2008). Viewed from humancentric perspectives, we need to address animal abuse because it is a sign of potential or actual human-to-human abuse.

In the case of domestic violence and animal abuse, 'The Link' needs to recognise that domestic violence does not just reflect a propensity for humans, particularly heterosexual men, to violate other humans. It must formally recognise that animals—in and of themselves—can be brutalised by domestic violence, as direct targets, pawns, and witnesses. In other words, instead of talking about links between domestic violence and animal abuse, we need to also discuss domestic violence experienced by animals. It may seem a pedantic and small change, but it has deep ramifications. Continuing to talk about 'links between domestic violence and animal abuse' frames the issue in such a way that the animal abuse is qualitatively different from the human-experienced abuse, that is, it is not domestic violence. In so doing it ignores many other links, including the links between deteriorating health and well-being for both human and animal domestic violence survivors, if they are forced to reside apart from each other for lengthy periods, post-separation from violent perpetrators. There are also links between love and abuse (see Chap. 4), links in-and-between different forms of abuse, and the links in-and-between victims and perpetrators—a subject we have not considered in this book.

Our position is to respect what 'The Link' has offered and appreciate how ground-breaking it was at the time, but nevertheless push for it to become a more multi-dimensional concept that captures a wider range of intersecting phenomena. We cannot continue to position animals as an adjunct or precursor to violence experienced by humans. This is neither a fair nor an accurate representation of the phenomena. Explicating the links in-and-between human-animal abuse offers more conceptual possibilities for understanding how abuse can occur within, and condoned by, institutions. This includes institutions that implicitly support violence, most normatively displayed towards disenfranchised others. For instance, it allows us to more carefully appreciate how human hierarchies of superiority legitimise the domination and maltreatment of others, including humans described as animal-like, or constructed as pets, pests, wild, feral, dogs, bitches, and sluts. These are just some of the many possible examples highlighting the utility of 'The Link' adopting an intersectional understanding of abuse.

Feminist Intersectionality

Intersectionality is a concept used by critical scholars to refer to interlocking systems of (traditionally) human oppression (see Mattsson 2014). In the original conception of intersectionality, Crenshaw (1989, 1991) showed how understanding the intersection of devalued social identities (such as black, female, and working-class) can produce much more sophisticated insights about oppression, but also how these different identities can pull the person in different directions, producing divided loyalties. Crenshaw's (1991, 1241) intersectionality focused on black women's experience of race, class, and gender, and laid the ground for deeper understandings of how to respond to oppression. For example, where systems of race, gender, and class domination converge, as they do in the experiences of battered women of colour, intervention strategies based solely on the experiences of women who do not share the same class or race backgrounds and therefore face different obstacles will be of limited help. Crenshaw (1991) also rightly points out that attempts to reproduce stereotypes about particular oppressed groups can obscure our recognition of and responses to the social problems that afflict them. She uses the example of domestic violence in black communities to highlight her point: "the real terror experienced daily by minority women is routinely concealed in a misguided (though perhaps understandable) attempt to forestall racial stereotyping" (Crenshaw 1991, 1256).

Since its original conception by Crenshaw (1989, 1991), intersectionality has been extended to include oppression by species (Birke 2012; Deckha 2008), as well as interlocking experiences of unearned privilege. Much of this work has been undertaken by ecofeminists who identify the links between the oppression of nature (and thus other species) and the oppression of women. As Twine (2010, 399–400) points out,

> ecofeminism has been from its outset about theorising an intersection between the co-positioning of 'women' and 'nature', but then also developed into a more multi-dimensional account of intersectionality … The agenda of ecofeminists such as Carol J. Adams and Josephine Donovan in juxtaposing 'animals' and 'women' is not the debasement of women but the explication of relations of power that intersect gender and species.

This is important to all animals, not just those who serve the role of companions to humans, as their devalued political positioning and relative absence of rights have been ignored for too long. As Birke (2012, 153–4) suggests, until recently "discussions of intersectionality have tended to disregard non-humans, rarely considering how human power is materially constituted (including being constituted through the bodies of non-humans)." Yet we need to take care that including species oppression in conceptions of intersectionality is not done solely to understand human oppression. As indicated earlier, positing that some groups of humans are more animalistic or closer to nature has been (and continues to be) a particularly effective tactic to legitimate their marginalisation and oppression. As Deckha (2008, 249) notes, the human/animal dichotomy can be used to bolster hierarchies among humans, with the lower ranked groups positioned as closer to animals than those with more social standing: "Our identities and experiences are not just gendered or racialized but are also determined by our species status and the fact that we are culturally marked as human. More importantly – and this is the point I wish to stress – experiences of gender, race, ability etc., are often based on and take shape through the speciesist ideas of humanness vis-à-vis animality". Understood through this extended version of intersectionality, 'The Link' exists not for the primary benefit of humans but for humans and animals equally. As Birke (2012, 154) points out, the inclusion of speciesism rounds out intersectionality, and in deeply embodied ways: "What bringing (some) animals into this discussion does, it seems to me, is precisely to emphasise intercorporeality, the sharing across boundaries of bodily responses, and the bringing into being of mutually affected physiologies."

A central problem including speciesism in intersectionality, however, is how to do so in meaningful ways. How might other animals be seen, heard, represented in political structures that humans have designed for themselves? If we emphasise intersectionality in research and theorising and seek to understand the multiple and complex ways that power structures cut across or complement each other, then we must recognise where other species are situated in those power structures (Birke 2012, 152). This leads to difficult questions, such as how can speciesism be incorporated into our understanding of intersectionality without recreating hierarchies among and between species? For instance, how do we avoid reproducing categories of animals based on human assessments of their value (to humans)? We don't have all the answer here; however, we do believe that part of the solution is in valuing animals in their own right, not simply due to their relationships with humans. And this means valuing all animals, not simply those who live in close proximity to us.

Taking Animal Abuse Seriously

At this point it might seem as if we have strayed away from our original purpose: to explore the connections between human and companion animal experiences of domestic violence and to do so in relation to the concept of rescue. As abstract and philosophical as this discussion of intersectionality might sound, it is important because it speaks to the foundations on which 'pets,' 'companion animals,' and other 'animals' are built. Because as tempting as it might be to adopt commonsensical ideas about pets, livestock, wildlife, and humans, it is a trap that must be avoided. Just as feminists argued about women not being 'added on' to structures and systems that privilege men, animals cannot be tacked onto existing renditions of intersectionality. To think about domestic relationships of violence and abuse without due consideration of how power relations are materially, psychologically, culturally, and socially shaped is to miss the point. Worse still, denuding the context of power relations in domestic violence is misleading and creates distortions in thinking. And to include notions of power without attending to species undermines the concept of intersectionality: we cannot ignore the fact that humans are not just placed in relation to but in opposition with animals.

> Animal is a slippery word, conflating enormous diversity. Whatever its meaning in biology (as species classified within the kingdom Animalia, including humans), its most common colloquial use is as counterpoint to the human … The primary problem, then, in thinking about "animals" is the enormous difficulty of escaping from a word, which does enormous cultural work in maintaining human exceptionalism. (Birke 2012, 150)

Under the human/animal dichotomy, animals are an indistinct, amorphous group of beings. The same might be said about humans but what distinguishes humans from animals is the assumed superiority of humans—however devalued in or excommunicated from society—over all other beings. 'They,' animals, stand in contrast to the 'us' humans attribute to themselves.

Most relevant to this book is the subcategory of companion animal. However, the mechanisms that place animals as secondary to humans are also those that allow us to make distinctions about other animals, for example, between 'companion' animal and 'food/meat' species. In other words, who is included and excluded in this classification is not self-evident. Chickens are an example of a species that may be classed as livestock for eggs and meat or as pets. Sometimes chickens are initially considered pets and then turned into meat as their egg production wanes. Dogs are constituted as pets in some cultures, food in others. Cows are sacred in some cultures, whereas in others, their skin lines sofas, and their flesh becomes meat eaten at barbeques.

The potential overlap of experience between different categories of oppression, and for that matter privilege, is not just obvious but important to recognise if we are to understand how unearned systems of privilege continue to flourish, in turn, producing oppressive regimes for those who are devalued. For instance, if you assume that all dogs are 'just dogs' requiring man's dominion to flourish, then the individuality of the dog will not seriously matter. His/her/their temperament, preferences, and potential deviations from expected species-related (or in many cases breed-related) assumptions will be ignored or viewed through pre-existing conventions. It cannot be any other way if, 'at the end of the day, a dog is just a dog.' If, however, we accept that the mechanisms that make a dog 'just a dog' are similar, if not the same, as those that devalue all marginalised groups then there is a need to take animal harm seriously, not just in its own right but as part of understanding these [mechanisms]. This means considering the frameworks and theorising we use to understand violence and oppression. In the case of the current argument, it means [acknowledging] that animals are also victims of domestic violence.

Conclusion

Taking the abuse of animals seriously means giving due consideration to the needs, rights, and interests of companion animals caught up in domestically violent situations, whether as witnesses or targets of abuse. It also means recognising companion animals' rights during and after human-perpetrated abusive episodes—episodes that have the potential to precipitate momentous changes to their living arrangements, including those surrendered to kill-shelters. As we explained, 'The Link' was initially designed to show how animal abuse by humans was an indicator, precursor, or 'red flag' to humans abusing other humans more than it was to protect the rights of animals. More inclusive and expansive conceptualisations of 'The Link' offer us the opportunity to track the web of possible connections between human and animal abuse, but also both groups' susceptibility to the pain of abuse through love and loyalty. Similarly, intersectionality offers us different ways to think about linked oppressions, marginalisation, and violence to both humans and other species. Extending our conceptualisations of human and other animal relations is imperative if we are to challenge and change attitudes and practices that support domestic violence across species lines. To quote Adams (2007, 22), "Violence against people and against animals is interdependent. Caring about both is required."

References

Adams, C. (2007). The war on compassion. In J. Donovan & C. Adams (Eds.), *The feminist care tradition in animal ethics: A reader* (pp. 21–36). New York: Columbia University Press.

Allen, M., Gallagher, B., & Jones, B. (2006). Domestic violence and the abuse of pets: Researching the link and its implications in Ireland. *Social Work in Action, 18*, 167–181.

Arluke, A., & Irvine, L. (2017). Physical cruelty of companion animals. In J. Maher, H. Pierpoint, & P. Beirne (Eds.), *The Palgrave international handbook of animal abuse studies* (pp. 39–57). London: Palgrave Macmillan.

Ascione, F. R. (1998). Battered women's reports of their partners' and their children's cruelty to animals. *Journal of Emotional Abuse, 1*, 119–133.

Ascione, F., Weber, C., & Wood, D. (1997). The abuse of animals and domestic violence: A national survey of shelters for women who are battered. *Society & Animals, 5*, 205–218.

Ascione, F., Weber, C. V., Thompson, T. M., Heath, J., Maruyama, M., & Hayashi, K. (2007). Battered pets and domestic violence: Animal abuse reported by women experiencing intimate partner violence and by nonabused women. *Violence Against Women, 14*(4), 354–373.

Australian Bureau of Statistics. (2013). *Personal safety*, Australia, 2012, cat no. 4906.0.

Australian Bureau of Statistics. (2014). *One in four women has experienced emotional abuse by a partner*, Media Release 27 June 2014.

Benjamin, J. (2013). *The bonds of love: Psychoanalysis, feminism, & the problem of domination*. New York: Pantheon.

Birke, L. (2012). Unnamed others: How can thinking about "animals" matter to feminist theorising? *NORA-Nordic Journal of Feminist and Gender Research, 20*(2), 148–157.

Black, M. C., Basile, K. C., Breiding, M. J., Smith, S. G., Walters, M. L., Merrick, M. T., Chen, J., & Stevens, M. (2011). *The national intimate partner and sexual violence survey: 2010 summary report.* Retrieved February 6, 2018, from http://www.cdc.gov/violenceprevention/pdf/nisvs_report2010-a.pdf

Burczycka, M., & Conroy, S. (2017). *Family violence in Canada: A statistical profile,* 2015, Juristat. Retrieved February 6, 2018, from http://www.statcan.gc.ca/pub/85-002-x/2017001/article/14698-eng.pdf

Campbell, W. K., Rudich, E. A., & Sedikides, C. (2002). Narcissism, self-esteem, and the positivity of self-views: Two portraits of self-love. *Personality and Social Psychology Bulletin, 28*(3), 358–368.

Campo, M., & Tayton, S. (2015). *Domestic and family violence in regional, rural and remote communities, an overview of key issues.* Australian Institute of Family Studies. Retrieved March 3, 2018, from https://aifs.gov.au/cfca/publications/domestic-and-family-violence-regional-rural-and-remote-communities

Carlisle-Frank, P., Frank, J. M., & Nielsen, L. (2004). Selective battering of the family pet. *Anthrozoös, 17*(1), 26–41.

Carnes, P. (2013). *Don't call it love: Recovery from sexual addiction.* New York: Bantam.

Charles, N. (2017). Written and spoken words: Representations of animals and intimacy. *The Sociological Review, 65*(1), 117–133.

Crenshaw, K. (1989). Demarginalizing the intersection of race and sex: A black feminist critique of antidiscrimination doctrine, feminist theory and antiracist politics. *University of Chicago Legal Forum, 140,* 139.

Crenshaw, K. (1991). Mapping the margins: Intersectionality, identity politics, and violence against women of color. *Stanford Law Review, 43,* 1241–1299.

Currie, C. (2006). Animal cruelty by children exposed to domestic violence. *Child Abuse & Neglect, 30,* 425–435.

Deckha, M. (2008). Intersectionality and posthumanist visions of equality. *Wisconsin Journal of Law, Gender, & Society, 23,* 249.

DeGue, S., & DiLillo, D. (2009). Is animal cruelty a 'red flag' for family violence? Investigating co-occurring violence toward children, partners, and pets. *Journal of Interpersonal Violence, 24*(6), 1036–1056.

Donovan, C., & Hester, M. (2014). *Domestic violence and sexuality: What's love got to do with it?* Bristol: Polity Press.

EUFRA: European Union Agency for Fundamental Rights. (2015). *Violence against women: AN EU-wide survey*. Retrieved February 6, 2018, from http://fra.europa.eu/en/publication/2014/violence-against-women-eu-wide-survey-main-results-report

Faver, C. A., & Strand, E. B. (2003). To leave or to stay? Battered women's concern for vulnerable pets. *Journal of Interpersonal Violence, 18*(12), 1367–1377.

Fisher, H. E., Aron, A., & Brown, L. L. (2006). Romantic love: A mammalian brain system for mate choice. *Philosophical Transactions of the Royal Society, B: Biological Sciences, 361*(1476), 2173–2186.

Fitzgerald, A. J. (2007). "They gave me a reason to live": The protective effects of companion animals on the suicidality of abused women. *Humanity and Society, 31*(4), 355–378.

Fletcher, G. J., Simpson, J. A., Campbell, L., & Overall, N. C. (2015). Pair-bonding, romantic love, and evolution: The curious case of Homo sapiens. *Perspectives on Psychological Science, 10*(1), 20–36.

Fraser, H. (2005). Women, love, and intimacy "gone wrong": Fire, wind, and ice. *Affilia, 20*(1), 10–20.

Fraser, H. (2008). *In the name of love, women's narratives of love and abuse*. Toronto: Women's Press.

Fraser, H., Taylor, N., & Morley, C. (2017). Social work and cross-species care: An intersectional perspective on ethics, principles and practices. In B. Pease et al. (Eds.), *Critical ethics of care in social work: Transforming the politics of caring* (pp. 229–240). London: Routledge.

Frieze, I. H. (2005). *Hurting the one you love: Violence in relationships*. Belmont: Wadsworth Publishing Company.

Fromm, E. (2000). *The art of loving: The centennial edition*. London: A&C Black.

Geffner, R., Igelmen, R., & Zellner, J. (2003). *The effects of intimate partner violence on children*. London: Routledge.

Green, P., & Gullone, E. (2005). Knowledge and attitudes of Australian veterinarians to animal abuse and interpersonal violence. *Australian Veterinary Journal, 83*, 619–625.

Hartman, C., Hageman, T., Williams, J. H., Mary, J. S., & Ascione, F. R. (2016). Exploring empathy and callous – unemotional traits as predictors of animal abuse perpetrated by children exposed to intimate partner violence. *Journal of Interpersonal Violence*, online first, https://doi.org/10.1177/0886260516660971

Hearn, J. (2012). The sociological significance of domestic violence: Tensions, paradoxes and implications. *Current Sociology, 61*(2), 152–170.

Illouz, E. (1997). *Consuming the romantic utopia: Love and the cultural contradictions of capitalism.* Berkeley: University of California Press.

Kearney, M. H. (2001). Enduring love: A grounded formal theory of women's experience of domestic violence. *Research in Nursing & Health, 24*(4), 270–282.

Kelly, L. (1996). When does the speaking profit us?: Reflections on the challenges of developing feminist perspectives on abuse and violence by women. In M. Hester, L. Kelly, & J. Radford (Eds.), *Women, violence and male power: Feminist research, activism and practice* (pp. 34–50). Buckingham: Open University Press.

Kelly, L., & Westmarland, N. (2016). Naming and defining 'domestic violence': Lessons from research with violent men. *Feminist Review, 112*, 113–127.

Lawson, J. (2012). Sociological theories of intimate partner violence. *Journal of Human Behavior in the Social Environment, 22*(5), 572–590.

Lynch, K., Baker, J., Lyons, M., Feeley, M., Hanlon, N., Walsh, J., & Cantillon, S. (2016). *Affective equality: Love, care and injustice.* New York: Springer.

Mattsson, T. (2014). Intersectionality as a useful tool: Anti-oppressive social work and critical reflection. *Affilia, 29*(1), 8–17.

Mayock, P., Bretherton, J., & Baptista, I. (2016). Women's homelessness and domestic violence: (In)visible interactions. In P. Mayock & J. Bretherton (Eds.), *Women's homelessness in Europe* (pp. 127–154). London: Palgrave Macmillan.

McDonald, S., Collins, E., Nicotera, N., Hageman, T., Ascione, F., Williams, J., & Graham-Bermann, S. (2015). Children's experiences of companion animal maltreatment in households characterised by intimate partner violence. *Child Abuse and Neglect, 50*, 116–127.

Milaniak, I., & Widom, C. S. (2015). Does child abuse and neglect increase risk for perpetration of violence inside and outside the home? *Psychology of Violence, 5*(3), 246–255.

Monsalve, S., Ferreira, F., & Garcia, R. (2017). The connection between animal abuse and interpersonal violence: A review from the veterinary perspective. *Research in Veterinary Science, 114*, 18–26.

Mouzos, J., & Rushforth, C. (2003). *Family homicide in Australia* (Trends and issues in crime and criminal justice, No. 255, pp. 1–6). The Australian Institute of Criminology. Retrieved March 3, 2018, from https://aic.gov.au/publications/tandi/tandi255

Newberry, M. (2017). Pets in danger: Exploring the link between domestic violence and animal abuse. *Aggression and Violent Behavior, 34,* 273–281.

Noller, P. (1996). What is this thing called love? Defining the love that supports marriage and family. *Personal Relationships, 3*(1), 97–115.

Oord, T. J. (2005). The love racket: Defining love and agape for the love-and-science research program. *Zygon, 40*(4), 919–938.

Øverlien, C. (2010). Children exposed to domestic violence: Conclusions from the literature and challenges ahead. *Journal of Social Work, 10*(1), 80–97.

Radway, J. A. ([1984] 2009). Reading the romance: Women, patriarchy, and popular literature. Chapel Hill: University of North Carolina Press.

Rigsby, B. (1999). Aboriginal people, spirituality and the traditional ownership of land. *International Journal of Social Economics, 26*(7/8/9), 963–976.

RSPCA. (2013). Royal Society for the Prevention of Cruelty to Animals. *Prosecutions Department annual report 2013.* Retrieved March 3, 2018, from http://www.rspca.org.uk/ImageLocator/LocateAsset?asset=document&assetI d=1232735296611&mode=prd

Shaver, P. R., Morgan, H. J., & Wu, S. (1996). Is love a "basic" emotion? *Personal Relationships, 3*(1), 81–96.

Simmons, C., & Lehmann, P. (2007). Exploring the link between pet abuse and controlling behaviors in violent relationships. *Journal of Interpersonal Violence, 22*(9), 1211–1222.

Singer, E. A. (1916). Love and loyalty. *The Philosophical Review, 25*(3), 456–465.

Sternberg, R. J. (1995). Love as a story. *Journal of Social and Personal Relationships, 12*(4), 541–546.

Taylor, N., & Signal, T. (2008). Throwing the baby out with the bathwater: Towards a sociology of the human-animal abuse 'Link'? *Sociological Research Online, 13*(1), http://www.socresonline.org.uk/13/1/2.html

Tiplady, C., Walsh, D., & Phillips, C. (2012). Intimate partner violence and companion animal welfare. *Australian Veterinary Journal, 90*(1–2), 48–53.

Twine, R. (2010). Intersectional disgust? Animals and (eco)feminism. *Feminism & Psychology, 20*(3), 397–406.

Velleman, J. D. (1999). Love as a moral emotion. *Ethics, 109*(2), 338–374.

Volant, A. M., Johnson, J. A., Gullone, E., & Coleman, G. J. (2008). The relationship between domestic violence and animal abuse. *Journal of Interpersonal Violence, 23*(9), 1277–1295.

Walsh, A. (1991). *The science of love: Understanding love and its effects on mind and body.* Buffalo: Prometheus Books.

Wetherell, M. (1995). Romantic discourse and feminist analysis: Interrogating investment, power and desire. In C. Kitzinger & S. Wilson (Eds.), *Feminism and discourse: Psychological perspectives* (pp. 128–144). London: Sage.

Wood, J. T. (2001). The normalization of violence in heterosexual romantic relationships: Women's narratives of love and violence. *Journal of Social and Personal Relationships, 18*(2), 239–261.

Wuerch, M., Giesbrecht, C., Price, J., Knutson, T., & Wach, F. (2017). Examining the relationship between intimate partner violence and concern for animal care and safekeeping. *Journal of Interpersonal Violence*, online first, https://doi.org/10.1177/0886260517700618

Yllö, K. (2005). Through a feminist lens: Gender, diversity and violence: Extending the feminist framework. In D. Loseke, R. Gelles, & M. Cavanaugh (Eds.), *Current controversies on family violence* (pp. 19–34). Thousand Oaks: Sage.

Zlotnick, C., Johnson, J., Kohn, R., Vicente, B., Rioseco, P., & Saldivia, S. (2006). Epidemiology of trauma, post-traumatic stress disorder (PTSD) and co-morbid disorders in Chile. *Psychological Medicine, 36*(11), 1523–1533.

Fig. 3.1 Woman with a white bull terrier

3

What We Choose to Hear: Researching Human-Animal Violence

Introduction

Throughout the book we use data from multiple projects (see Chap. 1 for outlines), but because of its focus, we draw most heavily from the project *Loving You, Loving Me: Companion Animals and Domestic Violence.* In this chapter we focus on research theories and methods reflecting on how we framed and designed the study, recruited participants, and made sense of the findings. We also explore some of the deeper epistemological questions about our decision to focus on women and animal victims/survivors of domestic violence. This project brought us into close physical and emotional proximity with (cisgender, heterosexual) women and animal survivors of domestic violence, and involved several ethical and methodological considerations. As we discuss in more detail later, our primary research partnership was with a local women's service: Northern Domestic Violence Service (NDVS). NDVS mostly provides support to women on low incomes in the outer suburbs of South Australia. Most NDVS clients face multiple social problems not exclusively related to domestic violence, such as gender, racial and/or class discrimination, chronic poverty, housing insecurity, and unstable employment possibilities.

© The Author(s) 2019
N. Taylor, H. Fraser, *Companion Animals and Domestic Violence*, Palgrave Studies in Animals and Social Problems, https://doi.org/10.1007/978-3-030-04125-0_3

Our pathway into learning more about what it means to be subjected to domestic violence and then have to rebuild post-separation focuses on the experiences of cisgendered, heterosexual women living in the outer suburbs of South Australia. Yet, there are many ways into discussions of domestic violence, including how it affects a wide variety of groups. Equally legitimate pathways would have been to work directly with children and young people, or elders, or people who identify as gender or sexually diverse, and/or heterosexual men abused by women intimates. In other studies, questions might legitimately be raised about the possibility of some victims also being perpetrators of violence, whether as retaliatory violence or through the abuse of others (such as children or elders). Still other possibilities relate to working exclusively with perpetrators of domestic violence. Many other possible lines and methods of inquiry are valid and necessary. We chose our particular route because the NDVS, who agreed to partner with us, assisted with the recruitment and support participants before and after our home visits where we conducted our interviews. Our interest in the NDVS was also based on their ten-year history of offering housing for adult and child victims *and their companion animals* fleeing domestic violence. We wanted to both highlight the service and research what it meant to the women to be able to remain with their animal companions.

Framing the Questions, Designing the Research

As explained in Chap. 1, we had several motivations for writing this book. Three of them were to (1) draw attention to the links between domestic violence and animal abuse, (2) bring into the mainstream discussions of domestic violence experienced by human and non-human victims/survivors, and (3) provide a platform for human victims/survivors of domestic violence to express their love for their animal companions, gratitude for the support they provide/d, and concern about the effects domestic violence has, and may (continue to) have, on both them and the animals they are connected to.

While recruiting from the women's service client-base we could have specified we only wanted to work with women from a specific ethno-cultural background, such as Indigenous women, or with women who had experienced homelessness due to domestic violence, or those who have children who were also affected by the violence and abuse. We decided to work with women and their companion animals, especially those who the service assessed in the first instance as willing and able to handle an invitation into our study. We had no knowledge of who would be participating in our study prior to meeting them: that we ended up with nine heterosexual women under 50 years from a mix of Indigenous and non-Indigenous backgrounds, most of whom had children, reflected the main demographic serviced by the support provider and who were willing to engage with us. The nine women and their individual interview transcripts have been instrumental in shaping much of the content of this book.

While this might sound straightforward, there are many political, phil-osophical, and methodological considerations to be navigated. For instance, it is important to acknowledge the debates about whether (or not) discussions are usefully framed through the lens of victims/survivors and perpetrators, with recognition given to the possibility that victim/perpetrator categories may overlap or digress, in that they may not neatly align with assumptions about women as victims and men as perpetrators. Questions have also been asked about the utility of the meta-narrative of (heterosexual) men abusing (heterosexual) women—and their children—in private homes considering the negative impact such a heteronormative meta-narrative can have for those who do not fit (see, e.g., Donovan and Hester 2014 in relation to the experiences of violence by LGBTIQ people). Others have pointed to the risks of not retaining a (binary) gender analysis of likely victims and perpetrators, given the scale of the problem affects so many heterosexual women as victims/survivors with heterosexual men as perpetrators. From this vantage point, there is the risk that to disconnect completely from albeit assumed heteronormative dynamics of domestic violence, the ongoing gendered patterns of violence and abuse may be missed or ignored (Kelly and Westmarland 2016).

Putting the spotlight on women's experiences of domestic violence carries the risk of wrongfully conflating women with the identity of victim; an identity which now carries much shame. There are also risks associated with (over)generalisation, across groups of low-income women, for example. Most of our data is derived from a small study in one geographical region. Apart from the staff involved in the project, nine women service clients agreed to be interviewed. We know that nine women do not constitute a random, representative sample, even for heterosexual women on low incomes affected by domestic violence living in the northern suburbs of South Australia. That is not our point or purpose. Our aim is to provide qualitative insights about the experiences of a specific group of victims/survivors—in this instance, heterosexual women aged in their middle years, living in one region of South Australia and clients of one particular women's service. These reported experiences and our interpretations and representations may—or may not—resonate with others' domestic violence experiences. Irrespectively, they matter both individually and as a collection of reported experiences.

Still others have (rightly) insisted that since domestic violence also interacts with other social identities, relating to class, ethnicity, religion, and geographical locations, more attention needs to be paid to subgroups of men and women. This is especially so with racialised and impoverished groups whose wider experiences of violence (on the streets, at school and work, etc.) are likely to be qualitatively different from white, middle-class experiences of domestic violence, where private arrangements in housing, therapy, medical care, and so on can be more easily and discreetly accessed. This is not to say that domestic violence is less significant for people with a better social and financial status, but it is to say that the help-seeking attempts and resources on offer are likely to be quite different depending on an individual's social and financial background. As we will show in later chapters, help-seeking and support for recovering from domestic violence vary greatly and are affected by changing government priorities and provisions and the level and flow of funding to domestic violence programmes and related services.

At the national and international level, the priority of various social and political problems, such as domestic violence, is apparent not just from the periodic media attention given but the budgets allocated to stem, redress, and prevent the problem. Compared to many areas of government spending, such as tax incentives and breaks for (big) business and growing military budgets, domestic violence is not being treated with the urgency and intensive resourcing required. In Australia and elsewhere, domestic violence and animal abuse both still tend to be marginalised areas of study, positioned as less urgent and less important to fund ways to address than other forms of violence, such as international terrorism (see Pain 2014).

Domestic Violence Is More Than a 'Women's Issue'

It is neither new nor coincidental to accord lesser importance to violence done to marginalised groups such as animals and women. Historically, domestic violence has been classified as 'a woman's issue,' a construction that has usefully drawn attention to the fact that many women are subjected to domestic violence, but also one that has allowed for the trivialisation and/or dismissal of domestic violence as a significant social and political problem. This is compounded by a discursive framing of domestic violence as a 'private' issue, a construction of the problem that still circulates despite decades of feminist work contesting it as such. As Walby et al. point out, "the prioritization of different forms of violence is not a simple given but is socially variable and influenced by media and other social practices" (2014, 190). In other words, what we choose to focus research on, what we choose to hear throughout the research process— and how we decide to actually do the research—are the result of complex socio-economic-political variables. And when these variables come into play, marginalised groups tend to suffer. This is the case with both domestic violence and animal abuse, studies of which are relegated to the sidelines of various mainstream disciplines and discourses. Challenging this positioning was one of the motivations for writing this book.

We knew that domestic violence and animal abuse are difficult areas to research in terms of accessing people willing and able to discuss them. Shame, victim blaming, and injunctions that victims should (just) leave/ get out/escape are common experiences of domestic violence and can interfere with people's willingness to disclose personal experiences. According to Berns (2009, 2–3),

Domestic violence has become a social problem *about the victims*. Most media stories focus on the victim. The victim is celebrated for having the courage to leave the abusive relationship or, conversely, blamed for staying and letting the abuse continue. He or she is accused of provoking the abuse and held responsible for ending the abuse. The victim is told to take back his or her power and refuse to tolerate the abuse anymore. Though not every story covers all these themes, together they represent the dominant portrayal of domestic violence in popular media. This focus may help build support for programs that help victims of domestic violence. However, it does little to develop public understanding of the social context of violence and may impede social change that could prevent violence.

As we argue throughout this book, part of developing public understanding of the social context of violence requires us to turn our attention to the many companion animals caught up in abuse and the living conditions of the humans they are associated with. Key to this is highlighting the issue and doing so in such a way that people are willing to listen.

We therefore wanted to write an accessible piece of work that considered domestic violence and animal abuse as linked, conceptually and empirically. It needed to be a project (and subsequently a book) that emphasised not just abstract and conceptual ideas, but also the materialities of everyday lived experience. To achieve this, we knew it was important to dedicate time to *listening to* the voices of women and companion animals caught in these situations. From the outset we wanted to press for more time and resources to be spent researching and addressing these links and to validate the area as a legitimate focus for research, across methodologies and methods.

Designing the *Loving You, Loving Me* Project

The *Loving You, Loving Me* project was the outcome of collaboration between the two authors of this book, the NDVS in North Adelaide, South Australia, and Relationships Australia, South Australia (RASA, North). It was comprised of two equal parts: a community art and photo exhibition project (led by NDVS and RASA, North) and the research project led by researchers Fraser and Taylor. This involved interviews with nine women who lived with companion animals, had experienced domestic violence (towards them and/or their children and/or their companion animal), and who were interested in being interviewed for the project. NDVS and RASA managed the art and photo exhibit and we (Nik and Heather) managed the research component. The NDVS caseworkers approached the women on our behalf, and if the clients were interested in participating, the caseworkers passed their details along so we could make contact and set up the interviews. All the interviews, except one that took place on the NDVS grounds, occurred in the women's homes with their animals present.

The aims of the overall project were to:

1. Raise community awareness of the link between domestic/family violence for women, child, and companion animal survivors.
2. Explore the importance of human-animal connections for many people (adults and children, Indigenous and non-Indigenous) especially during family crises and/or while recovering from domestic abuse.
3. Recognise the existing work occurring in the northern suburbs of Adelaide that help to foster ongoing bonds with animals for women and children escaping domestic/family violence.
4. Design a project that would take into account the many ethical complexities of the work.
5. Focus on survivors' experiences and bonds with their animals.
6. Find a way to engage children without re-traumatising them. (This was done through the art/photo exhibition. We did not interview children for the project.)

The politics of voice and representation influenced the design of our study. Concern over the inclusion and exclusion of voices and realities led to our development of a project that gave primacy and space to women's stories of being abused and to our being "politically, personally and sociologically committed to listening seriously and respectfully to [their] experiential accounts" (Scott 1998, 4.1). However, this held its own tensions not least in terms of our own awareness that qualitative research is often seen to lack credibility. From a rigidly empirical perspective, one that values only large-scale quantitative research, qualitative studies involving small numbers of participants may be dismissed as lacking rigour and generalisability. Without the numbers, and statistical analyses of the numbers, representations of domestic violence studies using personal testimonies as data may be dismissed as anecdotal. We were also aware that our project might be seen to undo some of the quantitative (and thus more accepted) research about domestic violence and animal abuse, particularly if new ideas emerged. Then there was the tension of sidelining the animals, who for us were as much a part of the reason for this project as the women. Our compromise was to design the study with a visual component (the art and photo exhibition) so animals could at least be made physically visible in the project.

Framing the Project

We thought carefully about how to frame this research, for, as Lee and Renzetti point out, "the very fact that a researcher poses a particular theory or research question can have major social implications" (1993, 514). They give the example of how research on domestic violence for a long time has (misguidedly) focused on answering the question, "why do battered women stay with partners who abuse them?" This established "the parameters of the problem of spouse abuse in terms of the behaviour of battered women" (1993, 515). Mindful that the framing of a research project can have often unintended but nevertheless serious consequences, we wanted to be sure that the way we framed our research did not re-victimise the women (by ostensibly blaming them for not leaving) or position companion animals as 'tools' to be used as a 'red flag' (Ascione 2001) for identifying human to human violence, or as mechanisms to help humans recover after violence. Framing animals in such a way erases their own needs and interests as sentient beings discrete from humans and their interests. Neither of these renderings is acceptable to us. This is why we decided to focus on the strength of the bond between human and animal and how that might lead to mutual aid in recovery.

The choice of approach is feminist because feminist research acknowledges that "a fundamental link remains between listening to what people have to say about their lives and identifying patterns and relationships which expose the operations of power and oppression" (Scott 1998, 1.5). One difference between our work and much existing feminist work is that it includes other species in these patterns of power and oppression.[1] Another difference is our interest in feminist intersectionality, inclusive of speciesism, discussed in other chapters. Key to listening to what people have to say is being willing to hear their voices—voices that are often silenced by their marginalised positions, while also acknowledging that the women and animals in our study, "like all precarious subjects, are not voiceless; they are deliberately silenced" (Sayers 2016, 371) and therefore taking care to do our best to hear them. In the case of animals, we clearly couldn't make space to 'hear' their voices but we did develop the project as a partly visual one to ensure they were able to be present in some way. Visual representations of them and of the bond their humans have with them were thus a key part of our design.

Focusing on these connections allowed an exploration of the animal's experiences. We didn't feel that another study establishing that domestic violence and animal abuse co-occur was needed; there is plenty of evidence of this already (see Chap. 2 for an overview). Nor did we want to start from a position that necessarily sidelines the animals in the work. In fact, we wanted the very opposite—to foreground them, as much as any human-based inquiry can (see Hamilton and Taylor 2017), by focusing on the *reciprocal relationships* they have with the humans we talked to. This notion of reciprocity is key as it recognises the importance of the animal and his/her agency and 'personhood' in the relationship; in other words, they are *someone* not something in this reciprocal relationship with 'their' human. This desire influenced our choice of method.

Getting the Chance to Meet the Animals

We needed to be sure that the approach we took to this project allowed space to 'see' the animals, as well as 'hear' their stories and those of the humans they lived with (Taylor and Fraser 2018). This necessitated a qualitative approach. Beyond this, it also directed us to a narrative approach that allowed the women to tell not only their own stories but

---

[1] We acknowledge that there is a lot of good work in this area (see, e.g., Adams and Donovan 1996; Gaard 2012), but it still is not central to the majority of feminist works.

also their animals' stories. Therefore, while we had a list of interview questions and prompts, by and large we didn't follow them closely but allowed the narrative to unfold naturally with prompts from us only when the stories stalled or when we wanted specific information. In this respect our interviews were conversations—again by design, in part because this gave the participants some control but also levelled the playing field somewhat. It felt less like an interview by an academic of a participant and more like a conversation, if not between equals then at least between people who share a common concern for the animals in the room. As Oakley (1981, 40) pointed out in her seminal piece concerned with power inequities in research with women, traditionally conceived projects lead interviewers to "define the role of interviewees as subordinates; extracting information is more to be valued than yielding it; the convention of interviewer interviewee hierarchy is a rationalization of inequality; what is good for interviewers is not necessarily good for interviewees." As Oakley and others have gone on to point out, this approach is anathema to the idea of giving marginalised, vulnerable research participants a 'voice' and visibility. Taking a different—narrative—approach addresses some of these concerns by allowing participants to direct the conversation and highlight issues that are important to them, not to the interviewer. It also leads to a more intimate conversation that in turn generates better data (Oakley 1981, 2016).

We also tried to interview the women participants with their animals present wherever possible. As you will see as you read this book, we have attempted to include the animals as much as possible by describing their stories where we can, without breaking confidentiality or putting any of the (human or animal) participants at risk. We acknowledge that this is a compromise—that we are *making* the animals visible, that we are *speaking for* them, and that our attempts fall woefully short and might not be what they would choose to have us know, if that were possible. As Cudworth points out, we have to acknowledge the power inherent in such a strategy: "In speaking for companion animals, human companions demonstrate their intimacy – the animal Other is so familiar that human companions can know how they think and feel … This is however, a considerable power – the power to construct the identity for an animal in the human world which they inhabit" (2011, 40). Despite this limitation, however, it is more important to include animals—even in a limited capacity—than to exclude them altogether, given what such an exclusion signifies:

> we do not so much discover the natural world as we construct it … We impose our cultural and descriptive narratives on the world like templates, text creating text. So if it is a feature of all these story-making activities that nature's particularity, and especially animals' particularity, is obscured, then there is cause for concern among all of us who care for animals as individual entities and not abstractions. (Vance 1995, 163)

Despite the inadequacies of this method, we remain committed to the principles discussed in the introduction to this book, of species inclusivity and a deliberate focus on the animals in and of themselves not as an adjunct to the abuse, a coercive device at the hands of the perpetrators of violence, or as a tool to help the women and children heal post-abuse. We accept that the animals are all of these things and more, but we do not want to simply reduce them to only this. We want their experiences to be a central part of this book and of the stories of love, violence, abuse, and healing alongside the stories the women shared with us about themselves and their children.

While the project was originally designed to include the animals for the ideological reasons outlined above it had two other unexpected benefits. The first is that our own interactions with the animals when we arrived at the women's houses served as a gentle way into their homes and removed any of the awkwardness that can mark (the start of) fieldwork and interviews. For the vast majority of interviews, the women opened their doors to us with their cats and dogs in close proximity. For us it was easy to give their humans a cursory hello before saying hello to the animals, bending over to pat them, picking them up when they indicated they wanted us to do so, and spontaneously asking questions that so many of us who live with companion animals ask each other: Who is this? What's her name? How old is she? When did you get him? Is he always so friendly? And so on. This occurred before we had a chance to double-check consent forms with the women and start the audio-recorders, which means that we don't have these exchanged captured in the transcripts. Yet they were so important. Nearly all the women said that they warmed to us because of these responses. They could see that we 'got it' and were 'animal lovers' and so they spoke more openly to us about their bonds with their animals, as they did not feel silly.

The second unexpected benefit of having the animals present during the interviews was that they helped *us* to cope with what we were hearing. Listening to the recounting of trauma from survivors is emotionally gruelling. We were witness to tears, rage, sadness, and frustration. We also heard stories about animal abuse. Having the animal present, usually sitting on one of our laps or lying on the couch next to us demanding attention, helped. Their presence was soothing, and, in the cases where we heard about their abuse, seeing them (more or less) recovered and happy, helped. Two examples spring to mind vividly. One is of a small fox terrier (Max) who was clearly loved by the woman he lived with: whenever she talked about him during the interview she looked at him and smiled; when we arrived and sat down he jumped on the couch between us and demanded attention and while ostensibly making sure we were OK with that his human made it clear it was his house and he got to sit on the couch whether we liked it or not. As the interview unfolded—and it was one of our longer ones, approaching three hours—and the woman in question (Brianna) told of the years of terror she and her dog had lived through, the dog (Max) sat on Nik's knee and simply cuddled there for over an hour. On the way home, in our usual debriefing session, Nik remarked how she "wasn't sure I would have got through that without the dog." The other example was an interview with a woman and her dog (Maddie), a mid-sized bull breed cross who also decided to sit on the couch between us for the entirety of the interview. Throughout the afternoon as we talked with her human guardian, she would periodically raise her head to lick one of us (checking on us? Soothing us?) when the interview was tense. She also helped us maintain emotional equilibrium by providing humour by alternately snoring loudly or kicking us both (she had positioned herself so that back legs touched one of us and front legs touched the other) if we stopped stroking her. We aren't claiming here that she understood when we were struggling with the content of the interview, but we are acknowledging that her presence helped us enormously.

There are countless other examples of ways in which the animals sat with, comforted, soothed, and checked up on their human companions throughout the interviews we conducted. One dog, (Freddy) an English Bull terrier, who started the interview at Heather's feet getting tickles and cuddles instantly moved to his human companion's side, wedging himself between her and the couch at the first sign of her (the human's) distress, and there he remained throughout. The woman in question acknowledged that this was standard behaviour for him and that he always sought to comfort her when she was upset. This was something we heard and witnessed throughout the interviews. As one woman told us about her long-time companion cat, Harley, "Once I start crying and getting upset [he] would be right up on my shoulder. He's the one … that pulls me through, if I'm crying or anything, he'll be right there going 'mum, get back into the present.'" Seeing first-hand the care and comfort the animals offered, as well as experiencing it ourselves, was an invaluable part of this research project and we urge other researchers interested in human-animal relations to ensure, where possible, that the animals can be present. Even so, we were still left with concerns over the ethics of this kind of 'intrusive' research.

Listening to Stories: Intrusion and Discomfort

Feminist researchers have consistently been open, honest, and brave when considering the research processes that they have used and their place within them. Often this has led to difficult 'conversations' about subjectivity, positionality, and the potential for researchers to appropriate (subordinated) others' knowledges and cultural practices. Feminists have long recognised that no matter what is done by, to, or with whom, research is an inherently socio-political process, temporally and culturally bounded. This applies to quantitative and qualitative research. The politics of research apply irrespective of whether the research is done through or in affiliation with universities, governments, and community groups. Feminist dilemmas related to the politics of research span ethics, funding, staffing, research focus, design, recruitment, analysis, dissemination, and everything in between (see, e.g., Letherby 2003; Oakley 2005). From a feminist perspective, especially an intersectional one that appreciates the interface of all forms of (structural, systemic, and cultural) privilege and oppression, there are no single answers or solutions to these dilemmas because humans and their/our interactions are complex, interconnected, messy, and often elusive, making human experience and all other experiences reported by humans hard to meaningfully capture and disaggregate, complicating attempts to measure and qualify.

By their very definition, dilemmas may mean that they are irreconcilable. However, this does not give a free pass to researchers, feminist, or otherwise. Instead, the task is to give careful thought to all aspects of the research we undertake, so as to articulate an honest and accurate account of how we handled the dilemmas that emerged. We know that critical analysis begins well before the first research question is posed and is not something adopted post-collection of data. Ethical considerations do not begin and end with the university ethics committee's approval process, which we know have their own self-interests to promote (such as minimising risk, and protecting their reputation or brand).

To qualify as feminist researchers, we undertake research that is contextualised and critically reflexive. We are not just interested in loose, interesting questions about gender but questions that are social-justice oriented. Part of being a feminist researcher is an explicit commitment to being socially just. It means giving due thought to, rather than sidestepping or brushing over, hard questions such as, 'Where I am positioned in this research? What gives me the right to study a specified population and represent that population's experience/knowledge/customs? How might I foresee and manage the research processes in fair and decent ways? How might the research be used (and misused)?' Whether working with 'convenient samples' (such as white, middle-class university students) or groups designated 'hard to reach' (such as low-income women trying to rebuild their lives in the face of extensive domestic violation), questions must be asked about unintended negative possibilities of the work. This includes the common institutional pressures to do the research faster, leaner and with more (public) impact (see Fraser and Taylor 2016).

The challenge is to find ways to ethically and respectfully engage with others, including research with animals. For intersectional feminist researchers, serious attention must be given to considering the costs of research, particularly research that is intrusive and sensitive and involves vulnerable/oppressed/traumatised people (and potentially other species) recounting aspects of hard and hurtful experiences. A key question has to be 'is their involvement worth it?' Janet Finch has expressed this reflexive concern with participant well-being by stating, "my interviewees need to know how to protect themselves from people like me" (1993, 173). In our research with women victims/survivors of domestic violence and their companion animals, there were times when we felt similarly.

We approached this project with years of experience researching domestic violence and animal abuse, experience that included interviewing women victims/survivors of abuse. In addition, we have, between us, social work experience of working with abused and traumatised humans, and animal shelter experience of working with abused and traumatised animals. We realised that we could not think through every permutation of what might happen 'in the field.' This is the joy and the challenge of fieldwork, never knowing what you will be faced with. But we did put a lot of time into thinking through the recruitment and interview processes. We did this formally—through our institutional ethics committee application form—and informally—through long discussions with each other about our fears. For instance, we asked ourselves what we would do if we were faced with an animal still being abused by the participant's children. How would we ensure our own safety while in the home of women and children, including those whose abusers were still hunting them down and could arrive while we were there? We also thought through these issues with the help of the service providers who worked on this project with us. In hindsight, however, we didn't put enough consideration into the emotional toll the research might have on us, a point we return to later.

Working in Partnership with Local Support Services

Interviewing women victims/survivors of domestic violence in their homes, often in the presence of their companion animals is complex ethical, emotional, and political work. Access to women's services clients in

Australia is not given easily, nor should it be. Many levels of scrutiny exist to prevent women being re-traumatised by indifferent and/or inept researchers whose primary or only interest is to extract 'data' from de-identified subjects. To quote Carley Milich, one of the staff members with whom we worked closely over the 12 months of fieldwork,

> NDVS receives requests from others to work with our women much of the time—we agree that partnering with other agencies and raising awareness of domestic violence is important to ensuring our service remains sustainable, however for our women this is often not the first priority on their mind. For them, finding a house or making sure they have enough food in the cupboards is more important, than opening up to any stranger about their experiences. We therefore had to be canny in whom we would suggest for interviews with the researchers. [Carley, Northern Domestic Violence Services Children's Advocate]

Passion and commitment are hallmarks of much feminist research and ours was no exception. That we felt passionate about the subject and committed to using our knowledge and skills to design and implement a process that would be validating for participants was key to successfully navigating this project:

> I can say that the researchers' passion for animals was an absolute linchpin in helping the women reclaim their relationship with their pet. Their positive vocalisations, their direct address of the animal and the telling of their own experiences with animals made them plenty of fans – both animal and human. The women would then light up and unabashedly speak their own language of affection towards their animal, telling of their idiosyncratic behaviours of which the researchers knew EXACTLY what they were talking about. Before this, they would have been ridiculed for showing the animal any attention—namely, because the perpetrator saw the animal as a threat, something that kept the woman strong. [Carley, Northern Domestic Violence Services Children's Advocate]

As feminist researchers with personal experiences of domestic violence and many years of professional work in the area, we still needed to be given access, or entry into being able to invite women to participate in our study.

To do so, we needed to demonstrate not just our research expertise but also our humanity, as women who were not afraid to enter the inner worlds of domestic violence through the eyes of the women participants and the touch and physical interaction with their companion animals.

> Many of our women had barely been able to share their stories with us as the immediate support workers, such was their trauma and existing high level of risk. We as workers agreed that the chance to verbalise their experience with the researchers would no doubt be valuable, but in many cases perhaps not yet. The researchers and case managers therefore had to remain flexible and opportunistic, in identifying where a woman might be ready to talk. For some, it would be immediately after they had settled at our emergency accommodation site—with their pets in their care. [Carley, Northern Domestic Violence Services Children's Advocate]

We worked with both our personal ethics as feminist researchers and with the national and institutional guidelines to think through the issues. We made sure, for example, that we liaised closely with the women's domestic violence caseworkers to gauge which women we were interested but also in a position to talk to us psychologically.

> In some cases, however, a woman's emotional state would change from day to day, dependent on what stressors had popped up. It could be hard for them to commit to the interview process, particularly when the long-awaited time came around and a woman had since been hospitalised, often for mental health issues. [Carley, Northern Domestic Violence Services Children's Advocate]

Both in advance and during the interviews, we appreciated the possibility of re-traumatising the women through the interview process. It is near impossible to discuss domestic violence and companion animals without somehow referencing painful personal material,

> Sometimes their [women participants'] anxiety at the thought of speaking about the abuse had flared up that very morning and they'd ask to reschedule.... Good communication and pre-emptiveness was required, to alert them in due time of any changes that may have occurred for the client. [Northern Domestic Violence Services Children's Advocate]

All the women we interviewed had caseworkers. We made sure that a domestic violence caseworker was able to follow up with them within a 24-hour period to make sure they were OK post-interview. Again, this was possible due to the work of the staff at NDVS.

> Often my routine would be to note any new intakes that had arrived to the units with pets, then check in with their case manager. Between the two of us and our Housing Officer, we would mention to the women that the opportunity to meet with the researchers was there. Once they had agreed to be contacted, I would email the researchers with a short brief about the woman's current sense of coping, readiness for speaking about the abuse and the nature of their relationship with their pet – this would help the researchers with building rapport straight away, as they would already be familiar with the animals. [Carley, Northern Domestic Violence Services Children's Advocate]

These are relatively commonplace and well-used methods to ensure participant's safety and well-being and they are important in any research but especially in research into 'sensitive' topics. However, this does not mean to imply that all complexities were neatly and resolutely dealt with.

Following Lee and Renzetti (1993) we take sensitive research as meaning that which may be intrusive but add to this research addressing issues that may cause, or have previously caused, emotional distress and pain, particularly because they are issues considered private and/or lead to feelings of shame usually because they are not discussed openly with others (due to a whole host of reasons nothing to do with the individual experiencing the events). However, we sometimes felt the measures we had in place weren't enough. We would leave interviews, that sometimes went for two to three hours (participants could stop the interviews at any point without any penalty; the length was entirely dictated by them), emotionally wrung out after what we had heard and would then discuss with each other 'how must it feel for the woman who shared the story?' These were some of the moments when we wondered if we were doing more harm than good: when the participants would spend a good proportion of the interview in tears, switching between pain and anger; when they told us they had just taken Valium so they could cope with the interview they knew would be 'tough'; or when they told us they needed to lie down as we left. In spite of the women thanking us for visiting and taking the time to really hear what they were saying, we reflected on the possibility that they needed 'to know how to protect themselves from people like us.' It is one of the reasons we stopped conducting individual interviews after meeting with nine women. Another reason was that we already had so much material, which even at the time we intuitively knew was 'good data.'

Hearing and Representing 'Good Data'

The misgivings we had about asking the women to retell their stories were compounded when, despite our best efforts to come at the research both reflexively and ethically, there were times when we echoed Etherington's (1996 in Sampson et al. 2008) shock and discomfort that when hearing stories of trauma and terror we could still be thinking about how it was 'good' data. When we discussed this after the interviews, we realised we meant that it was *useful* and part of that sentiment was bound up in it being something we could use to draw much-needed attention to the issues involved in understanding and preventing domestic violence and animal abuse in the home. Even so, listening to someone's recount of trauma and thinking how 'good' it is in any terms signal a response that left us uncomfortable. We accept that some of this is because it goes against everything we are told—particularly as women—we should feel. That is, when we approached the 'data' analytically, instead of emotionally, there was a sense we were 'doing wrong.' Of course, acknowledging the analytical importance of the data did not mean we divorced ourselves from any empathy with the interviewees or even from an emotional response. There were times when we wished we could do this but emotions (our own and the participants) were an integral part of this project, something we discuss in more detail below.

We are not alone in feeling this ambiguity towards the research process, and the data we gathered. Sampson et al. (2008) asked researchers about the 'cost' of reflexive methods they used and noted that many qualitative, and particularly feminist, researchers shared the feelings we detail here. They also noted that some of their sample expressed frustration with the outcome of their research, that in its final forms of dissemination it might not actually do anything for the participants or even for the groups of people they represented. We also share this concern but have taken some steps to combat it. We are not suggesting these are infallible, rather we discuss it here as we think this is an increasingly important part of the research process, particularly when working critically in areas deemed 'unimportant' in a neoliberal world. Elsewhere, we have documented the importance of adopting strategies that allow us to get research out to the world despite the constraints of a neoliberal university that seeks to close down critical/political research with marginalised groups (Fraser and Taylor 2016) and we remain committed to including consideration of this in our work.

One of the strategies we used with our projects on domestic violence and animal abuse involved choosing where to publish. For example, we decided at the outset of this project that it would form much of the current book you are reading. This was deliberate as we felt a book would be both more accessible (generally, and to the women who participated in the study if they were interested) and allow us more latitude to explore the issues in depth and with a more politicised stance than a peer-reviewed journal might.[2] We also designed the project (as outlined earlier) so that it had an art exhibition alongside the interviews. This served several purposes: (1) it drew attention to the (often hidden) existence of domestic violence and animal abuse. People, including journalists who have power to reach diverse audiences, were interested in the bonds between human and animals the artworks expressed. The 'nice' photos (both in content and in artistic rendering) were a drawcard for the journalists and public spaces (museums, art galleries, etc.) that showed the works. (2) It worked as an incentive for the women, and their children, to take part in the exhibition and then hopefully in the interviews, although the two were not dependent and we made it clear women could participate in the art exhibition and not be expected to talk to us (and some decided to take this option). (3) It gave something (back) to the

---

[2] This is not to say we will not publish in journals, but that our first choice of outlets will be elsewhere.

women and children involved not only in terms of a nice experience working with volunteer photographers (from the local Mawson Lakes Photography Club) to create beautiful and lasting images of their cross-species families, but also in the form of copies of the images provided to them afterwards. This also had the added advantage of helping solidify their relationships with their caseworkers, who took the pictures to them, and shared their joy in them.

The Power of Feeling Understood

In some respects, some of our concerns were allayed by the women who spoke to us. As indicated earlier, they often told us—or their caseworkers or the children's advocate at a later point—how much they got out of the interview process and that they were motivated to take part because one of the aims of the project was to raise awareness about interlinked animal abuse and domestic violence and the need for services that allow women to remain with their animals. As one of our interviewees put it,

> A lot of people are afraid to leave because of where am I going to go, what services can actually take me with my animals … But what a difficult choice between a 15-year-old relationship with two loved ones in your family [her cats], or you and your son … That's why I'm doing this, because it's painful as all fuck but I will not let another person go through this. [Nolene]

We also heard from the women that participating in the project was worthwhile to them and they appreciated talking to people who understood the power of their bonds with their animals. They were also clear they wanted their voices to be heard when it came to letting professionals know that recognising animals are important to them as a source of support but also that animals are themselves affected by violent households:

> …to tell professionals … they really need to – not just by head knowledge but with a bit of open compassion to see exactly what these dogs or any dog or animal does for a person who's been traumatised in such a way that where the deep healing of the scars need to mend and that, but with an

animal it can bring so much more than what they see on the surface. They can see bruising, they can see the scars but what's going on inside … she can get by counselling but she can also get it by having a companion as such a dog or a cat. [Linda]

The focus on the animals was key here. As described above, the presence of the animals and our responses to them often legitimated our interest in this area to the women who participated, which, in turn, encouraged them to talk openly to us about their animals without feeling foolish.

Many of the women thus came out of the interview experience with high praise for the interviewers and an affirmed belief that they had done the right thing, by considering their pets' needs. From what I could tell, their demeanour would often change towards their animal, with new appreciation. Until then, as long as the animal was safe, that would be all the emotional support she could offer that animal whilst in crisis mode. This is what NDVS's policy of allowing animals enabled, in the very least. However, the interview rather often marked a new chapter in her recovery – one where she could enjoy the company of her animal and finally start to heal. [Carley, Northern Domestic Violence Services Children's Advocate]

Politics, Harm, and Emotions in Research Work

Despite this positive feedback concerns remained and these were not limited to concerns about the well-being of the participants. We also wondered about the effects of our own, political and ideological positioning in the research. We are both 'animal lovers,' living with companion animals in our personal lives and advocating for all animals in our professional lives and through the research we do on human-animal relations that often focuses on the way humans oppress other species (not limited to companion animals). And we are both survivors of domestic violence who have also been researching the areas of domestic violence and animal abuse for decades. Clearly, our own biographies are embroiled in our decisions about the work we do, including writing this book and the various research projects that underpin it.

Our feminist position necessitates that we are open about the ways our biographies and political positions might affect our work. However, with this reflexivity comes the fear of having work discredited by outing ourselves in any number of (supposedly) contentious areas: as survivors of domestic violence, and in one case of domestic violence-related animal abuse; as feminists; as working-class women; as animal advocates and vegans. No doubt there are those who will question the research we have done, perhaps this book we have written, using the tired old complaints of too much 'subjectivity' or too much 'emotion.' We accept this will happen and that it is *more likely* to happen because we are *women* studying both domestic violence and animals. The still-assumed 'private nature' of domestic violence and the emotional ties humans have with animal companions lend themselves to this kind of masculinist, positivist critique. Further adding fuel to the masculinist critique fire is our openness about our own histories and our own politics.

Being Personally Affected

Our feminist ideology demands that we make our positions clear and reflect upon them, as we acknowledge that some of the research we did for this book affected us personally (see Rager 2005 for a first-person account of the potential emotional costs of 'sensitive' research on the researcher). It was evident in our demeanour, for example. The drive to the interviews took about an hour and we would chat about the project and other work-related issues all the way there. On the way home, however, we noted long silences indicative of both our emotional exhaustion and our busy minds as we sought to process what we had heard. One of us (Nik) often had to come home and ask her (male) partner for an hour alone with the dogs she lives with while she sought to balance herself: the idea of talking about the interviews, even at the abstract level demanded by confidentiality, was too much, especially with a male,[3] and

---

[3] Discussing issues of domestic violence, and in fact any violence, with men is equally as important as hearing testimony from female victims of male violence. And it is something we both do regularly through our teaching and community presentation work. However, directly after these interviews Nik simply didn't want to excavate the gender politics involved.

she sought the emotional comfort that only animals can give—silent, non-judgemental and utterly undemanding. In talking about these responses—and others—we often reflected that we were echoing our participants' behaviour and seeking and gaining solace from our non-human companions. This led to a consideration of the toll of the work on those we share our lives with, particularly through the emotional work we often ask of other animals. We discuss this more thoroughly in Chap. 7 when we consider animals' work but raise it here to demonstrate how being attentive to our own emotions in the research process can lead to new insights.

In thinking through some of these issues we came to the conclusion, like Sampson et al. (2008, 930), that

> It is perhaps an inevitable corollary of close research relationships that we will experience vicarious hurt, particularly where we attend to the basic principles of a qualitative research paradigm increasingly influenced by feminist research principles … no pain, no gain. This is not just the price of qualitative research, it is the price of human understanding in our everyday lives and it is one which the evidence of our Inquiry suggests is broadly viewed by researchers as a price worth paying.

Furthermore, we think that these emotional ties, and 'costs,' can be a strength in research. Analysis of researcher's emotions as well as those of the participants can provide theoretical insights and lead to what Campbell (2002) calls "emotionally engaged research" (p. 123) defined as "valuing and utilising the kinds of knowledge that can be revealed through careful attention to the affective experiences of the researcher and the participants." Campbell makes clear that this kind of research is guided by an ethic of care—for the researchers, the project, and the participants which in our case we would extend to non-human participants by acknowledging the plight of animals caught in domestic violence situations. As Campbell argues, an ethic of care is bound to a reciprocal relationship, a relational commitment, and using this to guide our research projects allowed us to care about the women and animals involved and to care about, acknowledge, and seek to understand their reciprocal relationships. It also facilitates research designed to understand how we can address significant social problems like animal abuse and domestic violence in such a way as to respond to the needs of those experiencing them; "Caring involves attuning to the well-being of those affected by the research, and allowing that concern to guide the many decisions researchers make over the course of the project" (Campbell 2002, 128).

Notes on Critical Companion Animal Research

As we have made clear throughout this chapter, planning and executing research with women and companion animals who have been affected by domestic violence is a complex and emotional affair. The ethical permutations are many and require thought and strategy before going into the field. Even then, there are likely to be issues that cannot be preempted. In our case, one of these was a growing awareness that we might not be able to advocate, uncritically, for women and their companion animals to remain together in situations where one or both are affected by domestic violence. Throughout the study we became aware of animals surrendered for their own safety and were forced to conclude—with the women who did the surrendering—that at that point in their lives this seemed to be the best course of action. We also started to become aware of the emotional labour that many of the animals performed. And while some of our human participants acknowledged this could take a toll on the animals, some did not and rather saw their animals as healers and as therapists without recognising that they might have their own post-trauma needs, such as the need to be free from both the expectation to heal humans and exposure to certain human emotions. We discuss this more thoroughly in Chap. 7 but raise it here as it has (and still does) presented us with conflicting feelings: we don't want to feel we are 'betraying' the women who participated by not offering wholesale and unequivocal support for their remaining with their companion animals, but we also owe something to the animals themselves and so, ultimately, this is a difficult issue we need to raise.

A Compassionate and Critical Approach

In part, this issue came about because we took a compassionate yet critical approach to the study of animals in society, in both our broader research focusing on humans and animals outside of domestic violence situations, and in that specifically addressing linked violence. This is not an easy position to occupy as advocating for other species often puts us at odds with advocating for other humans, given the basis of human-animal relations are so often exploitative. This becomes even more complex when approaching research into our relations with companion animals, as most assume those relations are good for other animals. While this might be the case for many animals in domestic arrangements in the home with humans, it is not the case for all. Yet, researching companion animals from a critical perspective occupies a somewhat unique position. While there is much research on the species we keep as companions within mainstream human-animal fields—such as the growing volume of work on animal-assisted therapies, or on links between cruelty to companion animals and domestic violence and child abuse—there is much less written from a critical perspective. Critical perspectives tend to focus on animal species used for food and entertainment, otherwise seen as 'products.' In part, this is due to the predominance of political economy/Marxist theoretical positions adopted by those who do this work (e.g., Murray 2011). Those working in this area—quite accurately, we think—point towards the commodification of animals that occurs when they are considered human property from which to secure a profit. This position has lent itself to various analyses documenting the discursive, symbolic, and ideological construction of other animals as inferior that justifies the oppression and abuse they are subject to for humans to realise that profit.

We support this work and, in general, agree with the positions taken. However, we have noticed that it has given rise to a form of hierarchical thinking where work done on/for these commodified animals is considered more radical, more worthwhile. Perhaps this is because statistically there are more animals living under oppression, for example, the billions of hens packed into tiny cages stacked in dark, dank 'battery' barns, the thousands of sows trapped in gestation crates, unable to even turn around, or the millions of bobby calves killed days/hours after birth, considered 'wastage' by a dairy industry. Perhaps it is because the suffering of these animals is so deeply hidden 'in plain sight' by various ideological sleights of hand that normalise such abuse and oppression. Or perhaps it is because it is assumed that companion animals get a much better deal.

In many ways they do. Some—the lucky ones—live comfortable lives in homes with humans who love and care for them. But these species are also open to abuse—at an individual level by 'owners' who can ignore them, leave them tied in backyards for the entirety of their lives, or who deliberately inflict violence upon them. Structurally, too, these animals suffer from the overall commodification of animal species. Take, for instance, the dogs forced to live without any human interaction, in small, dirty cages, kept as breeding machines to satisfy the latest market trend in 'cavoodles' or other 'designer breed.' Also consider the close to 40,000 companion animals euthanised in Australia annually (RSPCA 2015–2016) or 1.5 million euthanised in the US, per year (ASPCA n.d.) because they are surplus to requirements, or have 'behavioural problems' caused by previous trauma, repeat surrender, or simple boredom due to being ignored. In a cruel irony, much of this euthanasia occurs in shelters, the very places set up to help these animals in the first place. And, even those who do live in 'good' homes, where they are cared for and loved, are still subject to having their behaviour controlled, so they can live in human spaces. They are, as Collard (2014) put it, "lively but never fully alive" as their choices are curtailed and their agency limited or denied altogether (Sutton and Taylor forthcoming).

Adopting the position of critical companion animal studies allows us to consider contentious issues such as these although, as we have made clear in this chapter, this is not without its challenges. It allows us to advocate on their behalf through our scholar-advocacy, and to extend the notion of research informed by a social justice perspective to them. Such an approach involves taking "a stand with/for those most adversely affected by unfair practices and discriminatory policies" which recognises that "research has a moral dimension that transcends technical goals and purposes" (Smith and McInerney 2011, 15). Such a stand can occur in day-to-day, home settings that offer us alternative models and stories about human-animal relationships. As White and Cudworth (2014) point out, when contemplating strategies of resistance, a local milieu should be sought, one which places particular emphasis on the roles and responsibilities of the individual and the community as having the potential to be(come) meaningful sites of resistance that can effectively challenge interspecies domination. The emphasis on the intimate connections, the intimate and meaningful connections that humans make with nonhuman animals, brings with it a welcome range of new possibilities and spaces for radical change. (203)

In other words, it is important to see our work highlighting the importance of animals to the women in our study, and the women's work in protecting their animals and participating in the study, as a form of bottom-up activism:

in the context of 'normalised' animal exploitation and (ab)use, this activism could easily become embedded in the regular and the everyday; this means not simply in consumer choices … Or decisions about which animal rights organizations to support, but also in more active, deliberate, and positive forms of engagement. (White and Cudworth 2014, 214–215)

Conclusion

Articulating and grappling with theories and methods of research are crucial elements to doing feminist research. In this chapter we explained why we elected to undertake a qualitative project using individual interviews with nine women clients of a South Australian domestic violence support service. We have also detailed how we attempted to include the animals—or at the very least a clear focus on them—in our research. Identifying not just our rationale for the decisions we made but also some of the important dilemmas we faced is intended to demonstrate our use of critical reflexivity and contextualise the interview material analysed in the following chapters. As we have indicated, interviewing women still (relatively) raw from separating from abusive partners, in their homes and alongside their companion animals, enabled a level of intimacy conducive to the provision of rich data for our study, but also involved the costs of sharing and bearing witness to painful, if not torturous experiences.

References

Adams, C., & Donovan, J. (Eds.). (1996). *Animals and women: Feminist theoretical explanations*. Durham: Duke University Press.

Ascione, F. R. (2001). *Animal abuse and youth violence. Juvenile justice bulletin*. Washington, DC: Department of Justice.

ASPCA. (n.d.). *Shelter intake and surrender: Pet statistics*. Retrieved August 12, 2018, from https://www.aspca.org/animal-homelessness/shelter-intake-and-surrender/pet-statistics

Berns, N. (2009). *Framing the victim: Domestic violence, media, and social problems*. New Brunswick/London: Transaction Publishers.

Campbell, R. (2002). *Emotionally involved: The impact of researching rape*. London: Routledge.

Collard, R. (2014). Putting animals back together, taking commodities apart. *Annals of the Association of American Geographers, 104*(1), 151–165.

Cudworth, E. (2011). *Social lives with other animals: Tales of sex, death and love*. London: Palgrave.

Donovan, C., & Hester, M. (2014). *Domestic violence and sexuality: What's love got to do with it*. Bristol: Policy Press.

Etherington, K. (1996). The counsellor as researcher: Boundary issues and critical, dilemmas. *British Journal of Guidance and Counselling, 24*(3), 339–346.

Finch, J. (1993). It's great to have someone to talk to: Ethics and politics of interviewing women. In M. Hammersley (Ed.), *Social research: Philosophy, politics, and practice* (pp. 166–180). London: Sage.

Fraser, H., & Taylor, N. (2016). *Neoliberalization, universities and the public intellectual: Species, gender and class in the production of knowledge*. London: Palgrave.

Gaard, G. (2012). Feminist animal studies in the U.S.: Bodies matter. *DEP – Deportate, Esuli e Profughe, 20*, 14–21.

Hamilton, L., & Taylor, N. (2017). *Ethnography after humanism: Power, politics and method in multi-species research*. London: Palgrave.

Kelly, L., & Westmarland, N. (2016). Naming and defining 'domestic violence': Lessons from research with violent men. *Feminist Review, 112*, 113–127.

Lee, R., & Renzetti, C. M. (1993). The problems of researching sensitive topics: An overview and introduction. In C. Renzetti & R. Lee (Eds.), *Researching sensitive topics* (pp. 3–13). London: Sage.

Letherby, G. (2003). *Feminist research in theory and practice*. Buckinghamshire: The Open University Press.

Murray, M. (2011). The underdog in history: Serfdom, slavery and species in the creation and development of capitalism. In N. Taylor & T. Signal (Eds.), *Theorising animals: Re-thinking Humanimal relations* (pp. 87–106). Boston/Leiden: Brill.

Oakley, A. (1981). Interviewing women: A contradiction in terms? In H. Roberts (Ed.), *Doing feminist research* (pp. 30–36). London: Routledge and Kegan Paul.

Oakley, A. (2005). *The Ann Oakley reader: Gender, women and social science*. Chicago: University of Chicago Press.

Oakley, A. (2016). Interviewing women again: Power, time and the gift. *Sociology, 50*(1), 195–213.

Pain, R. (2014). Everyday terrorism: Connecting domestic violence and global terrorism. *Progress in Human Geography, 38*(4), 531–550.

Rager, K. B. (2005). Self-care and the qualitative researcher: When data can break your heart. *Educational Researcher, 34*(4), 23–27.

Sampson, H., Bloor, M., & Fincham, B. (2008). A price worth paying? Considering the 'cost' of reflexive research methods and the influence of feminist ways of 'doing. *Sociology, 42*(5), 912–933.

Sayers, J. G. (2016). A report to an academy: On carnophallogocentrism, pigs and meat-writing. *Organization, 23*(3), 370–386.

Scott, S. (1998). Here be dragons: Researching the unbelievable, hearing the unthinkable. A feminist sociologist in uncharted territory. *Sociological Research Online, 3*(3), 1–12. http://www.socresonline.org.uk/3/3/1.html

Sutton, Z., & Taylor, N. (forthcoming). Between force and freedom: Place, space and animals-as-pet-commodities. In R. White et al. (Eds.), *Vegan geographies*. London: Routledge.

Taylor, N., & Fraser, H. (2018). Resisting sexism and speciesism in the social sciences: Using feminist, species-inclusive, visual methods to value the work of women and (other) animals. *Gender, Work and Organizations*, online first. https://doi.org/10.1111/gwao.12246

Vance, L. (1995). Beyond just-so stories: Animals, narrative and ethics. In C. Adams & J. Donovan (Eds.), *Animals and women: Feminist theoretical explorations* (pp. 163–191). Durham/London: Duke University Press.

Walby, S., Towers, J., & Francis, B. (2014). Mainstreaming domestic and gender-based violence into sociology and the criminology of violence. *The Sociological Review, 62*(S2), 187–214.

White, R. J., & Cudworth, E. (2014). Taking it to the streets: Challenging systems of domination from below. In A. Nocella, J. Sorenson, K. Socha, & A. Matsuoka (Eds.), *Defining critical animal studies: An intersectional social justice approach for liberation* (pp. 202–220). New York: Peter Lang.

Fig. 4.1 Black cat

4

Being Subjected to Domestic Violence: Empathic Love and Domination

Introduction

From personal experience and the professional work that we have done over the years, we know that family life is often full of paradoxes. Rather than being sites of comfort and refuge from the stresses of the 'outside world,' families may be dangerous, damaging, and painful places (Straus et al. 2017). This is not some bleak, jaded, or idiosyncratic view. Rather, it reflects the staggering rates of domestic violence, including the regular injuries and fatalities which suggest that the institution of family is not nearly as safe, protective and comforting as it might sound (Straus et al. 2017).

From the project, *Loving You, Loving Me: Companion Animals and Domestic Violence* (2016–2017) (see Chap. 3 for more details), we draw most of our illustrative examples. Extended excerpts from interviews with women survivors of abuse reiterate how dangerous domestic relationships can be, for both humans and animals. They show that even when constituted as part of the family, companion animals are at risk of being harmed in private homes—deliberately and unintentionally—and having that harm ignored. They are at risk of being surrendered, abandoned, or retained during human survivors' moves

© The Author(s) 2019
N. Taylor, H. Fraser, *Companion Animals and Domestic Violence*, Palgrave Studies in Animals and Social Problems, https://doi.org/10.1007/978-3-030-04125-0_4

into various housing arrangements but expected to repress the impact their experiences of domestic violence have had on them, to focus on helping their humans recover. This discussion continues in the following chapters.

However, family relationships can also be conducive to great experiences of love, affection, and generosity but also justice (Kleingeld and Anderson 2014). Within families, justice does not have to be placed in opposition to love:

> One of the central insights of feminism is that a concern with justice should not stop at the entrance to the home. Changes in laws and public policy certainly play a pivotal role in ongoing efforts to eliminate injustice within the family. But one should not neglect the importance of transforming family members' attitudes toward the pursuit of justice within the family. (Kleingeld and Anderson 2014, 11)

This chapter begins with a definition of love, then of the *empathic love* that humans and companion animals can feel for each other as family members. Our emphasis is placed on excerpts from interviews from the *Loving You* project, where the women spoke of their deeply felt connections with companion animals. Most emphasised the empathy and kindness they felt to and from their animal companions. Many understood that their relationships were—at least partially—reciprocal. This is followed by a discussion about women leaving home early due to abuse. Attention then turns to when adult love relationships turn abusive, to attempts victims made to keep the peace and threats to safety if they tried to escape. Led by the data, our emphasis is on the recognition of animal love and companionship when victims/survivors of domestic violence reach out for help, and the importance of helping (non-abusive) humans to maintain their relationships with companion animals in the aftermath of separation. From these examples we will also show that human–companion animal connections can be both life-affirming (also see Headey 1999) and life-sustaining. This is a discussion that continues in some form throughout the remaining chapters of the book.

Empathic Love, Companion Animals, and Family

Empathy is a prosocial activity that involves trying to see life and feel experiences through the eyes of others and adjusting responses to them on the basis of these perceptions and sensitivities (also see Fraser et al. 2017; Kossak 2015). *Interspecies empathy*, as it is sometimes called, can serve as a bridge in and between humans and animals, allowing some humans, especially those alienated and traumatised, to reconnect with other humans as well as other species (Fraser et al. 2017). Empathy with and for animals has been shown to have a wide range of benefits for children and animals alike, including improved recognition of needs and rights of those being empathised with (Taylor and Signal 2005).

Love is a contested term and experience. For some, especially the biomedically oriented, love is best understood through various measurements, and in relation to human physiology, such as neural processes, changes to blood pressure, pulse rates, and hormones. From some other accounts, such as evolutionary psychologists, love is ultimately about instincts and survival. For others, love is fundamentally about attachments, or the spiritual merging of two to become one, or the site of much-needed emotional labour, to 'make relationships work.' Moral conservatives often view love relationships in terms of good/evil, morality/immorality, and obligations/recklessness. Still others, such as philosophers and social theorists, read love as a socio-cultural phenomenon, wrapped up in historical, social conventions that shape how we language our experiences of love, and, in turn, construct them emotionally, cognitively, and materially (Fraser 1999a, 2008).

Our interest in love and empathy cuts across species and domains of experience including those who are violent. For us, love is a code word used to describe a myriad of experiences, feelings, connections, behaviours, expectations, thoughts, plans, fantasies, and social expectations (also see Fraser 2003, 2005, 2008). Love relationships can be biological and physical, sexual or asexual, based on emotions or the withholding of emotions—material, intellectual, spiritual, religious, and/or institutional. Interspecies love relationships are those that occur across species, such as between humans and dogs, dogs and cats, and cats and chickens. Rather than attempt to try to capture love and associated terms in a single definition or through measurements, our emphasis is on human–companion animal relationships of empathy, connection, and love (Fraser 2008). (To reiterate an earlier point, this excludes human-animal sexual relations as we regard beastiality as abuse not love).

Empathic love between humans and animals refers to ongoing, loving companionate relationships based on mutual regard and care, emotional attunement and affinity, as well as reciprocal responsiveness to each other's interests and welfare. Lori Gruen's (2015, 3) notion of entangled empathy is relevant here:

> Entangled empathy [is] a type of caring perception focused on attending to another's experience of wellbeing. An experiential process involving a blend of emotion and cognition in which we recognise we are in relationships with others and are called upon to be responsive and responsible in these relationships by attending to another's needs, interests, desires, vulnerabilities, hopes, and sensitivities.

Interdependent and interconnected, entangled empathy is concerned about both the 'I' and the 'us' in relationships extending well beyond reason and rationality, to include feelings and perceptions of well-being (Bekoff 2006; Kossak 2015; Munroe 2018).

Mutual recognition is crucial to empathic connections, empathic alliances, and empathic love, all of which overlap. *Empathic alliances* are those characterised by empathy, trust, loyalty, partnership, and, most importantly, solidarity (also see Coulter 2016). However, they stop short of the intensity of emotional connections associated with love and may occur at a distance, for example, the generalised care that humans can feel for animals oppressed in modern agribusiness practices. When applied to human service provision and to practitioners' approaches, empathic alliances stand in direct contrast to *heroic treatment*, which Breggin (1999) described as typically expert-driven, crisis-oriented, directive and authoritarian, helping relationships, rarely required but often assumed in human hierarchies of status, knowledge, and power. In other words, empathic alliances are inclined to be more egalitarian, collaborative, and appreciative to each other's emotional needs and sensitivities (also see Bekoff 2006; Munroe 2018).

Empathic love can grow from *empathic connection*, a notion that speaks to being moved by another's story, physical presence, or experience. It can happen across species (Bekoff 2006; Vining 2003) and can occur fleetingly, such as when strangers meet and feel for each other. In the case of animal companions, these connections can happen during meetings at animal adoption centres or animal foster carers' houses, at dog parks, and during chance encounters, and for some these connections become relationships of empathic love in the future. During these initial encounters, individual animals may capture humans' attention by approaching them, engaging in play, allowing them to stroke them, or pick them up. Conversely, they may evoke human empathy and an impulse towards rescue when they shy away, hide at the back, shake with anxiety and/or appear to be unduly small or weak (sometimes described as the 'runt of the litter'). As discussed in Chap. 5, these physical vulnerabilities and fear responses have direct relevance to domestic violence, not just for human victims/survivors but also for animals' experiences of domestic violence.

We are using the notion of *empathic love* in an attempt to show the power of animal companionship and most importantly to highlight the emotional sensitivities of animals, not just humans (also see Bekoff 2006; Coulter 2016; Vining 2003). This has been particularly important given we could not interview the animals as we did the humans in our projects. In social media there is a popular psychological human character type described as an *empath*, which is ordinarily disaggregated from gender and all other politics and contexts:

Empaths are highly sensitive, finely tuned instruments when it comes to emotions. They feel everything, sometimes to an extreme, and are less apt to intellectualise feelings. Intuition is the filter through which they experience the world. Empaths are naturally giving, spiritually attuned, and good listeners. If you want heart, empaths have got it. Through thick and thin, they're there for you, world-class nurturers.... If empaths are around peace and love, their bodies assimilate these and flourish. Negativity, though, often feels assaultive, exhausting. Thus, they're particularly easy marks for emotional vampires, whose fear or rage can ravage empaths. (https://drjudithorloff.com/how-to-know-if-youre-an-empath/)

While the popular construction of empaths has not included companion animals, our view is that it should do so. After all, it is companion animals who are less apt to intellectualise feelings, more inclined to nurture others, show loyalty 'through thick and thin,' and be 'easy marks for emotional vampires.' Even more than women, animal empaths are susceptible to having the emotional labour they perform, unrecognised or trivialised. If in conflict with human interests, companion animals' needs for 'peace and love' can be easily ignored. Seeing them as 'empaths' has the advantage of drawing attention to the negative impact human anger, anxiety, depression, and rage can have on them, as well as highlighting the work they do with and for humans (Coulter 2016). Exploring connections between gender, species, and empathy, Munroe (2018) reminds us that empathy can be exploited. When humans profess empathy for animals, improved treatment and living conditions do not always result. Munroe (2018) cites the example of Temple Grandin, the North American animal welfare specialist who helps to design 'more humane' methods for slaughterhouses (Munroe 2018).

Empathic Love and Domesticity

Empathic love often develops while sharing domestic space together. Domestic arrangements can produce not just close proximity but also some powerful entanglements particularly in the context of domestic violence, where the power inequalities between men and women, adults and children, and especially between humans and animals, is often more accentuated than in other households. The empathy, loyalty, and trust that come from companion animals are often cherished for being unconcerned with and oblivious to the human methods of ranking people and discriminating against them on the basis of gender, sexuality, class, race, age, ability, religion, and so on. What does matter is the mutual recognition—or the process of seeing each other and each other's needs (see, e.g., Taylor et al. 2018, forthcoming).

Human-animal relationships depend on *non-deliberative interactions*. Non-deliberative interactions go beyond words and are sensitive to place, touch, smell, and sound (see Lang 2016). Touch is a major component of animal companionship and may play a particular role in forging the relationship and in helping humans (and potentially animals, although less is known about this) recover from trauma and oppression. Abused individuals may not welcome touch or be able to physically touch others (Montgomery et al. 2015) at least during some periods of their recovery, even though much research points to the need for touch as a component of a healthy life, and its role in healing, particularly post-abuse (Ardiel and Rankin 2010; Westland 2011). It is unsurprising, then, that the embodied aspects of the relationship between companion animals and their humans can play a role in deepening empathic love and in helping both to heal post-abuse. However, similar to humans, companion animals may not find it pleasurable being touched, if such attention is not built on relationships of mutual trust and does not account for their needs and preferences. As it can be for humans, unwanted affection for animals can be distracting, unpleasant, frightening, and, in some cases, traumatic. Unwanted affection may place the target in the difficult position of having to find a way to reject these advances without offending or alienating. For companion animals, there is the risk that if they upset their 'owners,' necessities may be denied, such as food, shelter, and a clean place to toilet.

As well as touch, place, space, territory, and living arrangements all matter to interspecies relationships. Humans are not the only species to seek comfort from familiar, secure, and predictable surroundings (see Safina 2017). For humans and animal companions, daily routines occurring in material spaces often produce such comfort. Moving to a new house can incur several dangers, as the women we interviewed who lived with cats understood. Cats are notoriously reluctant to move geographical locations, especially if they are permitted outdoors, partly because of the careful negotiations they need to do with other animals, humans, and traffic in the neighbourhood. Adults, children, and companion animals can all find it difficult to adjust to new surroundings. As the women's testimonies show, there can be much stress involved in repeatedly moving residence, especially in the context of animals being prohibited (as in the use of temporary motels) and/or violent spouses pursuing the victims after they have escaped. Stress can negatively, not just positively, impact the affection victims of domestic violence (animal and human) feel and show to each other. As we will discuss, sometimes the (risk of) neglect of animals is not indicative of deliberate cruelty or indifference but a reflection of the overwhelming difficulties other (human) family members are facing.

To recap: embodied and physically interactive relationships of empathy in animal love and companionship can protect both parties but also make them vulnerable to each other's pain and hardship. Being emotionally attuned to one another can mean experiencing each other's misery and pain, not just joy and happiness. For the women we interviewed who reported growing up with companion animals as part of their families, there were fears expressed about animals being mistreated by others at home.

Growing Up Alongside Companion Animals

Cultural change has made the conceptualisation of 'pets' as loved family members more commonplace than unusual (Walsh 2009). This has also been reflected across several human-companion animal studies we have conducted. From focus groups, online stories, and individual interviews to questionnaires, no participants in our studies about companion animals indicated that they conceived of 'their' companion animals as traditional pets, that is, objects of affection to be used and discarded at will, without regard for the animals' own needs and interests. Only part of this can be explained (away) by the self-selected recruitment processes we have used, the focus of our questions and the tone of invitations to participate. Across so many human-companion animal studies (ours and several others), there is a clear message: animals can offer people not just companionship but *love* (see Archer 1997; Morrison 2007; Nicholas and Gullone 2001; Paul 2000). These interspecies love relationships are significant; participants have told us over and again that their love for 'their' companion animals is as important as the love they experience with other humans, and for some, even more so.

Growing up with companion animals as part of the family can be formative for children; animals are known to provide children with important forms of emotional support and security (Triebenbacher 1998; Walsh 2009). Being accepted or 'chosen' by an animal as a source of familial love and protection can feel deeply affirming for many humans, especially young people (Nicholas and Gullone 2001). From their interactions with companion animals, many children have learned how to respect others and life itself (Walsh 2009). Childhood relationships with companion animals can also shape developmental and lifestyle trajectories into old age. For instance, 30 years ago Netting et al. (1988) showed, in their study based in Arizona, there are two major factors explaining whether elderly people elect to live with companion animals as they age, the first is whether they have positive childhood memories of companion animals, and the second hinges on whether their housing arrangements allow it. All the women we interviewed for the *Loving You* project currently lived with companion animals, to some extent because they were able to live in pet-friendly supported accommodation, or because they had caseworkers who helped them advocate to private real estate agents and landlords that they were worthy of being trusted with rental properties. It is a point we return to in later chapters when we consider the importance of making (at least some) pet-friendly residential space for victims/survivors of domestic violence.

All but one woman in the *Loving You* project recalled childhoods involving companion animals at home. The exception was Brianna, the youngest woman we interviewed, who reported being raised by a vegan mother who objected to the domestication of animals and the treatment of animals as 'pets.' Today, Brianna is also vegan but lives with her young daughter, along with a small terrier (dog, Max) and a marmalade cat (Carla), both of whom provided much delight on our visit. For the other eight women we interviewed, all reported spending much time with companion animals during childhood and loving them in profoundly important ways. Sometimes children's empathy for animals is expressed through connections forged with 'underdogs' and championing their causes. Stella talked about "bringing all the [stray] dogs home," reflecting that reciprocal benefits can accrue to the humans and other animals that rescue each other, that is, humans rescuing otherwise unwanted and soon-to-be-euthanised shelter animals and shelter animals rescuing humans from their own reports of isolation, loneliness, anxiety, and depression (Fraser et al. 2017, 496).

Some of the women narrated stories about relationships with animals that endured across many years. Jacqui was a good example. She said, "Mum and

Dad got a dog called Jim, that we grew up with, and I actually had him in my wedding." The practice of including dogs as members of bridal parties and then posting beautifully composed photos about the events was something we noticed when several of our online participants posted photos of them in bridal gowns, kissing or holding the paw of their dogs for another project *What is it about animals?* When we met Jacqui, she was living with a young male collie-cross called Charlie, a beautiful, energetic, silky coated dog, who was fun to meet but also challenging. For instance, when we arrived and put our bags down he cocked his leg and scent marked one of them. After we sat down, he climbed on top of the sofa we were sitting in, walking over us, and winding himself around us during the interview. His distracting but entirely friendly behaviour was punctuated with licks and what appeared to be 'grins.' Even so, we accept that his behaviour would be challenging for some, as it seemed to be for Jacqui, who spoke of her concerns about neighbours complaining about his barking.

In her mid-30s, Allison was living with her young son and dog, Freddy, in supported housing when we interviewed her. She recalled the love and comfort she felt from and for the companion animals with whom she had grown up:

> We had a cat then and a blue tongue lizard and a dog called Louie Armstrong, a black terrier cross. He lived until he was 21 that dog … He, he ended up with my grandparents but he was always my comfort whenever my parents were fighting … I'd sit with Louie no matter … And *so, I guess he was my family.* I learnt to talk to my animals I suppose, so I've never really once gone without a dog.

Allison spoke of growing up "learning to talk to [her] animals." She is not alone. Talking with, to, and about companion animals is a popular pastime, repeatedly illustrated as beneficial to a wide range of humans (see, e.g., Sams et al. 2006). This can include happy, fun stories but can also include discussions of pet loss and grief (see Donohue 2005). For some people, including young children, talking with/to/about animals may be the conversations of primary importance in their day-to-day lives (Sams et al. 2006).

While Allison conveyed a creative, energetic self with many friends, she also revealed her deep pain, ongoing trauma, and worrying feelings of alienation from others with whom she is ostensibly close. Like several other women we interviewed, Allison experienced abuse in childhood and left home as a young teenager. Subjected to many years of domestic violence while she was in young adulthood relationships, she disclosed self-medicating her emotional and physical pain, and she frequently self-harmed and was often suicidal.

For Linda, an Indigenous woman artist in her 40s who lived in transitional housing with a large bird, 'Pete,' there were other social problems to contend with including chronic poverty, institutional racism, and her own more recent addictions to gambling and alcohol and time spent in prison. When we interviewed Linda, she was—post prison release—optimistic and upbeat, and happily reconnected to her large, extended Indigenous family. When asked, she said that her first strong memory of loving a companion animal was of Zac, a little dog that she grew up with, who her parents said was 'hers':

> Well my pet was called Zac. He was a little bitser [mixed breed] dog. He was my dog, he was bought for me as a young kid. And as growing up I was – I lived in a home of domestic violence so I know for me that my Zac was, was just my best companion, my best friend, everything … Yeah. Everybody loved him. But he was mine. I was told he was mine. Settled with that and the thing with him he would which I loved coming home every day after school he'd wait out the front for me … And soon as he saw me getting closer he'd do like this spin around and then he'd shoot up the road and just jump all over me. Yeah, he was my best buddy. He was awesome … He was just like a human and that's what everybody said. He was just so loving. He was awesome.

Most companion animals require care and attention, which in turn may have positive effects on the human caregiver's sense of control and self-efficacy (Pachana et al. 2005). Linda reflected this in relation to her love of and care for her dog Zac:

> For me personally [having a dog growing up] was security … It was like I say a companion, friend. It brought for me a sense of even though I could see chaos and all that at home. It brought me a bit of stability and responsibility caring for something else.

Similar sentiments were expressed by Katrina about her dog called Ember, a Doberman identified in Katrina's story. In it, she shows how growing up experiences for children can be interwoven with companion animal relationships, and how they can be experienced as important forms of protection:

> [We] always had dogs in my family. We had Dobermans…. from a puppy … [we] … had a birthday cake and they [the dogs] were the centre of the family. Everything that we did revolved around the animals, [that] sort of thing. So, they [dogs] were a big part of our lives. They lived inside, they slept on the beds and they were family, so yeah … it was me and my brother [that] had our dog Ember. It was a bit different back then because kids used to be allowed out and –

Q: Roaming?
A: [Nods.] My dog would come everywhere with me, so every night we'd go down the playground together. We were best friends really. So yeah, he [dog] was my best friend growing up.
Q: Wow. When you think about going to the playground, how old were you?
A: Maybe eight to ten, about ten years old.
Q: They were different days then weren't they?
A: [Nods.]

Caring for another sentient being has also been shown to be helpful for groups (such as children, and older or frail individuals) who perceive themselves as primarily receiving care, rather than being able to provide it. Such an opportunity to provide meaningful care may help redress imbalances in support exchanges (reciprocity) in their relationships (Pachana et al. 2005, 108). However, Pachana et al. (2005) caution us not to forget that having the opportunity to interact with animals and care for companion animals is usually reflective of existing benefits and resources—opportunities often denied people on very low incomes, in nursing homes or boarding houses. In other words, the opportunity to live in close proximity to companion animals is not evenly distributed, with some groups denied the chance to do so.

Leaving Home Early Because of Abuse

For some of the women we interviewed, childhood abuse meant they had been forced to leave their family homes early. Leaving home early can be a frightening, alienating, and impoverishing experience for many (see Fraser 1999a). For some it generates a longing for a sense of family that can make them vulnerable to abuse, but particularly young women who are so often the targets of the injunction to form families through unions of romantic love (Fraser 1999a, 2003, 2005, 2008). Allison recognised this cultural injunction in her personal story when she said, "all I crave is a family and that's what I saw in Rich [ex-partner who abused her]." Among others, Allison illustrates how premature sexual partnering can occur for young people fleeing abusive family homes, and thrust in equally risky environments:

> I've always been an outcast I was out of home at 13 … I grew up with a Croatian bloke who was abused hard as a child and unfortunately, he carried that on [with me]. I was with him [as a sexual partner] for 8 to 9 years I think. But first I lived with the Hells Angels [motorcycle group] actually. They actually looked after me better than my own mum. They were actually a family unit—believe it or not. They had very old school morals, they just, they just did illegal activities. And they were actually solid people for me. Even years later I saw them and they were still, "Alli—if you ever need to be looked after or whatever you're part of the family." And then I met Danny and I moved straight in with him and became his little saviour … I certainly don't want the whole woe is me bullshit because I made the choice to stay, although if I did go he probably would have killed me … [Then] he realised I didn't give a fuck if I died. So, I would let him do the things that he used to do and then –
>
> Q: To you?
> A: Yeah lots and lots of stuff that I have flashbacks of now … Sometimes I'd be locked in a sunroom for 8 days with a dog bowl, things like that … I think I blocked out a lot of my childhood too because violence has always just been, I drank because of the violence and I used to do drugs because of violence, you know what I mean?
> Q: I do.

Alison's reference to the dog bowl in the sunroom for eight days came with no details and left us in silent contemplation hours after we had completed the interview. The crossover of ill treatment of women and dogs is self-evident. Debased and presumably kept hostage, Allison's attempt to flee domestic violence in her childhood home had cruelly resulted in her experiencing even more extreme violence.

Many young people are homeless due to abuse in family homes (Cooper 2016; Fraser 1999b). Historically and today, demand for supported accommodation often outstrips supply and many young people run the risk of having to 'couch surf' or 'sleep rough.' Both can be precarious, not just in terms of having possessions stolen but also being exploited, attacked, molested, and otherwise abused. Homelessness due to abuse has potentially serious consequences for all aspects of life, demonstrated, for example, through the life chances of young people in or leaving foster care, a group still susceptible to an adulthood of (further) violation, unemployment, homelessness, unsupported trauma histories, addictions, and imprisonment (Fraser and Seymour 2017). As so many young people discover, across the spectrum of genders and sexualities, leaving abusive homes can mean entering equally or even more violent contexts, where trading for resources can sometimes mean sexual exploitation and manipulation (Fraser and Seymour 2017). It can also mean having to leave behind beloved companion animals (Coorey and Coorey-Ewings 2018).

Katrina is another example of a woman growing up with companion animals and leaving home early due to abuse, but in her case, she had the opportunity to maintain connections with her dogs:

> I left home quite young, we had a dysfunctional family and I was out of the house I think I was about fourteen or fifteen and I had my own place through a government supported place; I think I was fifteen or sixteen and I had a dog then as well, so I got another Doberman and felt completely secure. If I didn't have the dog I would've felt empty and yeah, I wouldn't have felt safe at all. So yeah, Jackson was my second Doberman and yeah, he was my protector; he was just another human really … with black hair.

Q: Have you ever been without dogs for long periods?
A: No, I don't think so. Only the time that we spent homeless without Maddie. I really have never not had a dog in my life.

Katrina was not the only woman to have suggested that having a loyal companion at your side can be pleasurable at any time, but in the context of domestic violence and homelessness, can be more than a welcomed relief from the hardship fear and unpredictability.

When Adult Love Relationships Turn Abusive

Unexpected betrayals are common features of domestic violence. Many survivors recount how confusing domestic violence can be, how special and loving abusive partners can be before turning ugly, and how the abuse can creep in so unexpectedly (Fraser 1999a, 2008). Nadia was another woman who spoke about this:

> He [ex-partner] was really kind and friendly at first. When we first met, he was just so – I've never felt so special to someone, I've never felt like somebody loved me as much as him. He just, he was really wonderful that first couple of months. I thought he really understood me but obviously that was all not who he was … It almost, you don't even notice how bad it was getting until it got really bad. We moved house, into the house with our housemate and that's when things got awful. I thought that I was losing my mind, I really thought – oh my god I've gone completely crazy what is going on because he would say, "Oh this didn't happen how you remembered and that, that didn't happen and what I said was this." And I just, I'm someone who's always been pretty sure of myself and for the first time ever I was, I've gone mad, I've lost it, I really, I remember just sitting there thinking, this is what it's like to go crazy … How he was with me at the start is how he is with everyone else. I feel like I'm, I'm the only person who's seen that ugliness.

When we are hurt by the ones who purport to love us, the consequences can be shocking and profound, psychologically, physically, emotionally, financially, and spiritually. For some women, the abuse starts quickly after marriage. In the popular vernacular, spouses may be 'loyal to a fault,' especially if they have vowed to honour—and in many cases, obey their spouse—and stay with them 'til death do us part.' In the context of committed romantic heterosexual coupledom there are many inducements for women (and others) to not classify what they are experiencing as abuse, but instead reframe it as discrete and perhaps unintended incidents, disconnected from the overall quality of the relationship and hopes for the future (Fraser 1999a, 2003, 2008). While in hindsight it might appear obvious, it can be hard for victims of domestic violence to immediately recognise that what is happening to them is abuse. Katrina gave an example of this.

Q: So how long were you married before the abuse started?
A: To be honest, it started straight away.
Q: Did it [long and sombre silence].

We read the silence as hanging heavy because the implication is that if abuse starts early, departures by victims should be immediate. When they do not conform to this script for how victims should behave, much shame can be cast and internalised (Murray 2008). In part, this is due to 'public story' of domestic violence that constructs it as individual in nature, ensuring attention is moved away from more discomforting structural and cultural aspects and reasons for it. This is equally linked to the public stories narrated about love.

As we discussed in detail in Chap. 2, in popular culture and everyday life, clichés about love abound. Love is said to lift us up, rescue us from loneliness, deliver us a family, while helping us to heal from any past pain. In the popular imagination love can both rescue and transform us (Fraser 1999a). Not so popularly understood is that domestic violence relationships often, but not always, involve the coexistence of love and abuse, complicating how abuse is interpreted and dealt with (Fraser 2005, 2008; Straus et al. 2017). Also, not so popularly understood is that domestic violence can harm companion animals too, and not just those used as direct targets of abuse (Coorey and Coorey-Ewings 2018).

The Domestic Violation of Animal Companions

While domestic violence is enacted in diverse households and often hidden from public view, companion animals are highly likely to be picking up the tensions, hearing the explosions, witnessing the attacks and acts of submission by the humans they love. They are also likely to feel the aftermath and sense the misery at home, even if humans pretend the situation is otherwise.

In Chap. 2 we described how McDonald et al. (2016) interviewed 58 children who had experienced having their animals threatened, harmed, and in some cases killed. Linda's experience narrated below shows how her son witnessed his father try to kill their cat while pretending to do otherwise.

Q: Did he [ex-husband] ever do anything secretly to hurt them like an animal would just disappear or anything like that?

A: Well that's what he tried to do when my son saw what he'd done. He tried to do that because it was my daughter's cat and he tried to kill it but my son caught him.

Q: Right I see. He tried to kill the cat and get rid of the cat but pretend the cat had run off?

A: Yep and he done that, he's done it a couple of times actually.

Q: He gets the shits with an animal and kills it?

A: Yeah oh he gets the shits with me and he will take it out on them.

Linda understood her abusive husband's actions to be motivated by a desire to control her through the cats, that the cats were proxies for his rage. Her view echoes other research done in this area that demonstrates abusers use animals as a form of coercive control over their human partners (e.g., Adams 1996). Moving beyond the impact on the human alone, however, we attempted to imagine the terror experienced by the cats, who were suddenly targeted, captured, and killed. Our thoughts were also cast to the rest of the family who were to witness the arrival of subsequent cats, to love and bond with them (see Walsh 2009), only to have the whole sinister process repeated over and again. This weighed heavily on Linda.

Q: Was his [ex-husband] treatment of the animals any part of your deci-
      sion making about not wanting to be with him?
A: Yeah, yeah that and not wanting to get another animal while with
      him. Because I saw how he was [with the animals]. He [husband] was
      so dominant.... He's [son] lost a couple of animals in his time and
      I'm pretty sure he [son] vowed and declared that he would never have
      a – another pet.
Q: Because of the pain of losing them?
A: Yeah, yeah because – and seeing what his father had done and that
      sort of stuff.
Q: Did his father kill the animal?
A: Yeah.
Q: In front of him?
A: (Nods). *In front of him.*

Love relationships are popularly understood and often presented as a
balm to pain and grief (Fraser 1999a, 2008). Below, Linda describes
meeting her ex-husband when she was a teenager, a time when she was
raw from the grief of her brother dying:

I met him when I was what – I think it was a couple of weeks after I lost
my brother to suicide. He used to work with my cousin's boyfriend and he
brought him around, that's how I got to meet him. [However, we] made
five amazing children so yeah…

Q: So, not all bad?
A: No, no there's a lot of good – I've learnt a lot from him a lot of good
      things. He done a lot of good things with the kids and took us on
      good trips and camping and all that sort of stuff so it wasn't all bad.
      I mean I wasn't – I mean just – things just didn't work out. That's
      how I look at it now and I'm sure he's better off for it and I know I
      am. Heaps better off than what I was.

In spite of the extensive violence that her husband committed against
her, their children, and companion animals, Linda refused to cast him
only as a mistake or a blight on her life. She figured that their union
produced 'five amazing children,' whom she loves very deeply. For people unacquainted with the legacy of domestic abuse, it may come as a

surprise to learn that more than a few victims will still feel some form of love for perpetrators and hold hope for them to change, including those who have never shown remorse before (Fraser 2005).

Many domestic violence victims want the love relationships to continue free from the violence (Fraser 2005, 2008). As a result, trying to 'keep the peace' is a theme of many domestic violence victims' lives, human and animal. Sometimes this involves trying to ingratiate oneself to the abuser, as dogs sometimes do to angry 'owners,' including those unlikely to be placated but may even be further aggravated, as can occur when victims cower reflexively at sudden movements (also see Coorey and Coorey-Ewings 2018). Katrina described her attempts to placate and soothe her abusive partner:

> You know in the moment you just think 'I'm not going to rock the boat'. You're so busy walking on eggshells that you don't get your red flags anymore. You don't go, 'Hang on a sec. That's not normal!' You're just thinking, 'Let's downplay this, downplay that, or it's going to just blow up in my face' … Yeah, *keep the peace*. I used to say to my son all the time, 'Choose your battles wisely'. Now I look back and I think that's such a stupid thing to say because it just put us in a mode where we were walking on eggshells. We wouldn't – I wouldn't raise my voice to him, I was just constantly doing everything to keep the peace and it just –
>
> Q: Exhausting?
> A: It is. *It's so toxic – really, really toxic.*

Jacqui also realised she was expending much emotional labour trying to keep the peace with her abuser when she heard herself urge her young daughter to do the same:

> I would try and make sure that things wouldn't set him [abusive ex-partner] off. And I knew something, I knew I had to do something when, we were in the shopping centre with the kids and my daughter did something, and I heard myself saying "Please don't do that, dad's going to go off at me." And I'm like, "Oh my god, I can't do this, look what I'm doing to my child." *Do you know what I mean?*
>
> Q: I do, my mother used to say it to me.

Our response to Jacqui's fear of unwittingly colluding with her abuser was designed to convey that her response was not idiosyncratic, nor a reflection of her deficits, but reflective of the coercive control many abusers deploy, which can corrode victims' capacity to not internalise responsibility for the abuse occurring.

For some domestic violence victims, it is not just that trust that has been broken and that acts of domination can feel suffocating. They can also feel exploited, sometimes only realised after they have separated. Katrina described it as a feeling of being 'sucked dry':

> It's been hard, it's been a hard more than anything, a shock to – because I'm a giver and that's why he was attracted to me in the first place, *he sucked me dry and I just kept giving and giving and giving.* So, when you leave somebody and you've given so much of yourself and they immediately turn around and try and destroy your reputation it hurts you in a place where you didn't even know existed…

Similar to many other women we interviewed, Katrina also cursed herself for continuing to give so much of herself to a man whom she now saw had no intention of showing her mutual respect and empathy. There is also a risk—if not the intention—that domestic violence can 'break the [victim's] spirit.' This can include abuse that is strange, hard to read but nevertheless debilitating, as indicated in Allison's excerpt below:

> I don't tell many people [about the domestic violence and its connection to mental illness] and they don't get it anyway. A lot of people think mental health is an excuse, but they don't, this was, they don't see me pulling my hair out like I do. Like here [points to section of her hair], all this is short because I pull my hair out. I used to have really long dreadlocks. That was to stop me from pulling my hair out and then Rich cut them when I was asleep.

Does having your dreadlocks cut by your partner while you sleep constitute a discrete incident of domestic violence? In our view the answer is yes, but for many it would not be so clear-cut; and for many victims, especially those holding hope that they can maintain their love relationships but rid it of the violence, the answer may be no. For many it will take multiple, repeated, and extensive abuse to prompt any contemplation of terminating the relationships.

More Than 'Incidents' of Abuse

In Chap. 2 we described the problems associated with seeing domestic violence in terms of 'incidents' (whether one-off or a series), rather than as relationships of power, control, and domination. To quote Kelly and Westmarland (2016, 114), "It is precisely the repetition, and the web of various forms of power and control used by perpetrators, that entraps women in abusive relationships." All the women's stories pointed to the ongoing nature of the abuse they experienced, recounting specific incidents but placing it within a much wider context of ongoing abuse.

Forms of Coercive Control

Stark (2007) defines coercive control as strategically gendered, oppressive conduct designed to achieve male privilege by dominating partners and evoking their fear, abusing their rights while withholding resources. Stark (2007) argued for an understanding of domestic violence that sees "woman battering from the standpoint of its survivors as a course of calculated, malevolent conduct deployed almost exclusively by men to dominate individual women by interweaving repeated physical abuse with three equally important tactics: intimidation, isolation and control" (p. 5). Foregrounding Pain's (2014) call to see domestic violence and abuse as 'everyday terrorism,' Stark noted that the main harm inflicted upon women by coercive control is political in that it reflects a deprivation of rights and resources central to citizenship and personhood. He also drew comparisons with other "capture or course-of-conduct" crimes like kidnapping and harassment where perpetrators "use various means to hurt, humiliate, intimidate, exploit, isolate, and dominate their victims" (p. 5).

Hegemonic masculinity is relevant to coercive control demonstrated in many of the heterosexual relationships recounted to us. For example, Katrina described how all members other than 'the man of the house' were cast as naturally inferior:

> he [abusive ex-partner] doesn't have respect for animals. He's been brought up very differently. He's been brought up in a country environment on a farm killing animals for food. *His first job was at the abattoirs*, so his idea of – I don't even think he knows what empathy means, but he has no compassion for animals whatsoever. They're merely things to serve us or to be eaten you know what I mean? They're not our equals, they're just –
>
> Q: They're objects?
> A: *Yeah,* they're just objects. So, he actually used to get quite pissed off if I wanted her [dog] inside. I mean I've grown up completely differently, our dogs are our family members, they sleep with us, they cuddle us, they lick our face. His idea of an animal was she should be outside, so there was a lot of friction there between what he expected of her and what I wanted her to be in the family … I think it was, *'I'm the man of the house, I'm going to dominate and everybody will cower down to me to make me feel like the king.'*

Katrina attributed part of the problem of her male ex-partner's treatment of her, their children, and companion animals to him working at an abattoir, where there is a strict hierarchy of value that literally speaks to who lives and who dies. Men, women, children, and animals are hierarchically ranked—in that order of status and value—undergirding the legitimacy of abusive patriarchal relations.

In the course of coercive control, sometimes extending for years or even decades, victims can become ill, physically and emotionally. Katrina reflected on the impact the abuse was having on her own health and that of her son's:

> I was getting sicker and sicker, my son was sick; we couldn't work out what was wrong with him, he had heart problems as a baby, so we automatically went back to his heart and they literally did scans from his head to his toe; epilepsy, his heart everything; could not find out what was wrong. He was

sort of having these seizures and it ends up that he was having migraines and it's another stress response ... And he was so – he missed out on most of year ten, most of year eleven because these migraines would have him vomiting for twenty days at a time ... And hospitalised, he's been on a drip probably more times than every adult I know put together, he has just got so sick with it and not even once – now I can go back and go holy shit, that was a stress response, but at the time I just could not figure it out.

Q: You couldn't see it?
A: I couldn't see it.

Below Nolene noted how emaciated she had become through the violence. However, first she described the sexual abuse perpetrated against her by her (then) partner, and his exploitation of information she had disclosed to him about prior experience of rape that led to a pregnancy:

He [abuser] was my first partner after I had ... The partner that I had before him, and I hadn't dated, I hadn't been with anyone for four years, raped me and got me pregnant. So, I was very low, I was still – I was still dealing with that. I did end up with post-traumatic stress with that.

Q: Was he sexually abusive to you too?
A: Mmhm. That's how I broke up with him.
Q: Was that the tipping point?
A: Mmhm.... I was 43 kilos when I left ... When we went to court one of the things that he [second abusive partner] subpoenaed was my medical information, inclusive of the five years before I had even got together with him, which was the information in regards to my rape [from first partner].

Using sensitive information against a person is a common tactic for domestic abusers who are able to exploit the privileges that come with intimacy, whether sexual and/or familial. A common next step is to then project blame onto victims, such as denying there has been any such misuse or exploitation and reconstructing any distress or anxiety expressed by victims, as evidence they are 'paranoid' or have 'gone crazy.' Nolene's stories illustrate this gaslighting process, including the withholding of money for groceries, which on its own may not constitute an 'incident' of violence but placed alongside the other coercive behaviours created a relationship of abuse:

> It [violence] escalated. It was a very slow erosion of – it was a very, very slow erosion of the self, the little – the little things that would go missing, the little gas lightings, the isolation, the covert attacks that ended up making me lose my job, that whole, oh well if we work together and – and then it was complete control of the finances, my finances, to the point that at the end I had to, I started up a business, just so I could get petrol money, so I could –

> Q: So, he was on a good income, but he just wasn't sharing any of it?
> A: Mmhm. I had to ask him for money for groceries.
> Q: So, when you were buying groceries: did he resent the money that was spent on the cats?
> A: *Oh yeah. Oh yeah.*

Not being given money for groceries can be an example of coercive control, and the expression of hostility shown towards paying for food for companion animals is another. Understanding domestic violence as ongoing, repeated coercive behaviours is crucial to including other animals in definitions and responses, along with the recognition that some kinds of abuse women and animals face are not explicitly illegal.

Similar to Nolene, Linda was another woman we interviewed who reported how her husband used her personal disclosures of past abuse against her. The pain of physical violence seemed preferable to the pain of emotional betrayals:

> I always said to him [abusive husband], "Look, I can cope a smack in the mouth but you start screwing with my mind and I know that's where – that's when you'll get me." [I was] Not thinking that he'd used it against me but I was speaking right into it wasn't I? I was telling him what to do to screw me over and he did … from day one you could say I was an open book. I let him know everything and has we progressed in our relationship I guarantee you everything that I said from back here he used right through as I've reflected over these – last year. I just – how he used every bit of information he got.

Conclusion

In this chapter, the focus was on empathic love, and the possibilities of domination for women and companion animals in domestic settings. Growing up with animals was the focus of the first section, with many of the stories the women narrated in the interviews showing how important companion animals can be for humans from a young age. As indicated all but one of the women we interviewed grew up with companion animals. For some of the women, domestic violence occurred in their childhood homes as well as their much later adult relationships. More than a few grew up in contexts of animal cruelty, and for some, these experiences consolidated their future connections with and attempts to protect companion animals. Several examples of being abused have been included to show how challenging these experiences can be, not just for the women's self-esteem but also for their own and their companion animals' physical and psychological survival. Stories about trying to escape the violence by moving out of their homes are part of this discussion, as are stories about the connections with their animals. These themes, particularly the importance of remaining together—for both humans and animals—are taken up in the next two chapters.

References

Adams, C. (1996). Woman battering and harm to animals. In C. Adams & J. Donovan (Eds.), *Animals and women: Feminist theoretical explanations* (pp. 55–84). Durham: Duke University Press.

Archer, J. (1997). Why do people love their pets? *Evolution and Human Behavior, 18*(4), 237–259.

Ardiel, E., & Rankin, C. (2010). The importance of touch in development. *Pediatric Child Health, 12*(6), 153–156.

Bekoff, M. (2006). Animal passions and beastly virtues: Cognitive ethology as the unifying science for understanding the subjective, emotional, empathic, and moral lives of animals. *Zygon, 41*(1), 71–104.

Breggin, P. R. (1999). *The heart of being helpful: Empathy and the creation of a healing presence*. London: Springer.

Cooper, H. (2016). How can we support young people in youth homelessness services in New South Wales who have experienced domestic and family violence? *Parity, 29*(10), 33–34.

Coorey, L., & Coorey-Ewings, C. (2018). Animal victims of domestic and family violence: Raising youth awareness. *Animal Studies Journal, 7*(1), 1–40.

Coulter, K. (2016). *Animals, work, and the promise of interspecies solidarity.* New York: Palgrave Macmillan.

Donohue, K. M. (2005). Pet loss: Implications for social work practice. *Social Work, 50*(2), 187–190.

Fraser, H. (1999a). She makes love just like a woman: Romantic love narratives and young women in state care. *Australian Social Work, 52*(4), 17–23.

Fraser, H. (1999b, July). Considering the needs of children who are exposed to domestic violence: A feminist perspective for practitioners. *Women Against Violence: An Australian Feminist Journal,* (6), 34–40.

Fraser, H. (2003). Narrating love and abuse in intimate relationships. *British Journal of Social Work, 33*(3), 273–290.

Fraser, H. (2005). Women, love, and intimacy "gone wrong": Fire, wind, and ice. *Affilia, 20*(1), 10–20.

Fraser, H. (2008). *In the name of love, women's narratives of love and abuse.* Toronto: Women's Press.

Fraser, H., & Seymour, K. (2017). *Understanding violence and abuse: An anti-oppressive practice perspective.* Toronto: Fernwood Publishing.

Fraser, H., Taylor, N., & Signal, T. (2017). Young people empathising with other animals: Reflections on an Australian RSPCA humane education program. *Aotearoa New Zealand Social Work, 29*(3), 5–16.

Gruen, L. (2015). *Entangled empathy: An alternative ethic for our relationships with animals.* New York: Lantern Books.

Headey, B. (1999). Health benefits and health cost savings due to pets: Preliminary estimates from an Australian national survey. *Social Indicators Research, 47*(2), 233–243.

Kelly, L., & Westmarland, N. (2016). Naming and defining 'domestic violence': Lessons from research with violent men. *Feminist Review, 112,* 113–127.

Kleingeld, P., & Anderson, J. (2014). Justice as a family value: How a commitment to fairness is compatible with love. *Hypatia, 29*(2), 320–336.

Kossak, M. (2015). *Attunement in expressive arts therapy: Toward an understanding of embodied empath.* Springfield: Charles C Thomas.

Lang, N. C. (2016). Nondeliberative forms of practice in social work: Artful, actional, analogic. *Social Work with Groups, 39*(2–3), 97–117.

McDonald, S. E., Graham-Bermann, S. A., Maternick, A., Ascione, F. R., & Williams, J. H. (2016). Patterns of adjustment among children exposed to intimate partner violence: A person-centered approach. *Journal of Child and Adolescent Trauma, 9*(2), 137–152.

Montgomery, E., Pope, C., & Rogers, J. (2015). The re-enactment of childhood sexual abuse in maternity care: A qualitative study. *BMC Pregnancy and Childbirth, 15*, 194–201.

Morrison, M. L. (2007). Health benefits of animal-assisted interventions. *Complementary Health Practice Review, 12*(1), 51–62.

Munroe, A. (2018). Ableism, speciesism, animals and autism: The devaluation of interspecies friendships. In L. Gruen & F. Probyn-Rapsey (Eds.), *Animaladies* (pp. 89–100). New York: Bloomsbury.

Murray, S. (2008). "Why doesn't she just leave?": Belonging, disruption and domestic violence. *Women's Studies International Forum, 31*(1), 65–72.

Netting, E. F., Wilson, C. C., & Fruge, C. (1988). Pet ownership and non-ownership among elderly in Arizona. *Anthrozoös, 2*(2), 125–132.

Nicholas, R. F., & Gullone, E. (2001). Cute and cuddly and a whole lot more? A call for empirical investigation into the therapeutic benefits of human–animal interaction for children. *Behaviour Change, 18*(2), 124–133.

Pachana, N. A., Ford, J. H., Andrew, B., & Dobson, A. J. (2005). Relations between companion animals and self-reported health in older women: Cause, effect or artifact? *International Journal of Behavioral Medicine, 12*(2), 103.

Pain, R. (2014). Everyday terrorism: Connecting domestic violence and global terrorism. *Progress in Human Geography, 38*(4), 531–550.

Paul, E. S. (2000). Love of pets and love of people. In A. Podberscek, E. S. Paul, & P. Serpell (Eds.), *Companion animals and us: Exploring the relationships between people and pets* (pp. 168–186). Cambridge: Cambridge University Press.

Safina, C. (2017). *Beyond words: What animals think and feel.* New York: Picador.

Sams, M. J., Fortney, E. V., & Willenbring, S. (2006). Occupational therapy incorporating animals for children with autism: A pilot investigation. *American Journal of Occupational Therapy, 60*(3), 268–274.

Stark, E. (2007). *Coercive control: How men entrap women in personal life.* New York: Oxford University Press.

Straus, M. A., Gelles, R. J., & Steinmetz, S. K. (2017). *Behind closed doors: Violence in the American family.* London: Routledge.

Taylor, N., & Signal, T. D. (2005). Empathy and attitudes to animals. *Anthrozoös, 18*(1), 18–27.

Taylor, N., Riggs, D., Donovan, C., Signal, T., & Fraser, H. (forthcoming). People of diverse genders and/or sexualities caring for and protecting animal companions in the context of domestic violence. *Violence Against Women*. First published November 18, 2018. https://journals.sagepub.com/doi/full/10.1177/1077801218809942.

Triebenbacher, S. L. (1998). Pets as transitional objects: Their role in children's emotional development. *Psychological Reports, 82*(1), 191–200.

Vining, J. (2003). The connection to other animals and caring for nature. *Human Ecology Review, 10*(2), 87–99.

Walsh, F. (2009). Human-animal bonds I: The relational significance of companion animals. *Family Process, 48*(4), 462–480.

Westland, G. (2011). Physical touch in psychotherapy: Why are we not touching more? *Body, Movement and Dance in Psychotherapy: An International Journal for Theory, Research and Practice, 6*(1), 17–29.

Fig. 5.1 Tortoiseshell cat

5

Foregrounding Companion Animals' Experiences of Domestic Violence

Introduction

In the course of everyday life, companion animals offer so much to the many humans who live with them. Most are loving family members who show loyalty and playful affection to the humans with whom they have bonded. However, many companion animals spend most, if not all, of their time in close quarters, in yards and houses, and—for some, such as rabbits, rats, snakes, and guinea pigs—in crates and cages. When, whether, and how much they will be fed, exercised, and properly cared for depend largely, if not entirely, on their human 'owners.' Whether they will have a chance to experience the natural environment, breathe the air outside, feel the earth beneath their feet, and perhaps roll in the grass, also largely depends on the treatment they receive from humans. In contemporary Australia as elsewhere, it is still legal to permanently contain animals with the barest of minimum of requirements. We say this not to induce guilt but to point out that the situation for companion animals even in 'good, happy homes' is already likely to be ridden with strictures that most humans do not have to endure.

© The Author(s) 2019
N. Taylor, H. Fraser, *Companion Animals and Domestic Violence*, Palgrave Studies in Animals and Social Problems, https://doi.org/10.1007/978-3-030-04125-0_5

As we explored in earlier chapters all animal companions are at risk of domestic violence. Recorded abuse against domesticated animals suggests dogs are most often targeted, although this could be the outcome of a lack of reporting of domestic violence to animals generally, and to species other than dogs specifically (Grugan 2018). The kinds of physical abuses visited on animals in domestic violence are similar to those inflicted on humans and include kicking, punching, hitting, and burning but also species-specific abuse such as abusive holding by the ears (Grugan 2018; Williams et al. 2008; Tiplady et al. 2012). As we will show in this chapter, these abuses and the many forms of emotional abuse (including neglect) perpetrated against animals can generate trauma that is difficult to recover from.

We start by considering the various effects domestic violence has on animals' physical and emotional health and well-being, as well as considering what happens to animals more broadly when humans leave domestically violence situations. We note that not all humans are able to take their animals with them, for instance, and these animals may be surrendered to shelters or friends and family. While this is often done with the animals' best interests—and usually their safety—in mind, it is not unproblematic. We then extend our argument that the domestic violence done to animals needs to be taken seriously before concluding with some practical suggestions for how we might better support animal victims of domestic violence.

Throughout this book we have been arguing that animals' experiences of domestic violence need to be recognised in their own right as well as alongside human experiences. Leading on from this in Chap. 2 we argued that current theorisation and conceptualisation of domestic violence need to be extended to animal companions. We develop this argument further in the current chapter where we concentrate solely on animal experiences of domestic violence. Because our primary aim is to centre the animal experience of domestic violence, we have included excerpts from transcripts illustrating some of the ways in which animals can be harmed. This data is emotionally intense and contains confronting accounts of real lives being brutalised. As researchers and as humans who have survived domestic violence, we know how details of abuse can be used to grab attention and sensationalise issues. Our intention is to do anything but this. We include this material not just because so little data of this kind is available but also because the public exposure of abuse has a long history of substantiating calls to action. Second-wave feminists who catalogued the abusive effects of patriarchy through wife-battering and father-daughter rape are good examples of how important it has been to put on the public record actual details of abuse.

However, this discussion of the mis/treatment of animal companions in domestic settings also calls for us to go beyond the obvious ones of abuse perpetrated upon other animals. Difficult issues arise when we centre the animal's experiences and needs and notice how they can be at odds with human needs. For example, we note that respondents to our various projects often had to leave their animals with their abusers or place their animals in other less than ideal circumstances. We do not raise such issues to further burden human victims of domestic violence with guilt, or to suggest that they acted 'wrongly.' We accept that they did what they could with limited resources. Instead, we raise these issues because to help animal victims of domestic violence (and likely help their humans too), we must acknowledge the problems and the gaps in service provision and their possible consequences—including that people and their animals are left in positions where they have to adapt and invent 'workarounds,' which by definition will be less than ideal. The majority of approaches to domestic violence (and indeed other social issues and problems) exclude animals, casting them as passive victims to human agency, if they are mentioned at all. In direct contrast to that, we are arguing for the recognition of the domestic violence done to animals, who we view not as two-dimensional passive victims but as agentic beings. Animal standpoint theory (AST) offers some key ideas to this conceptualisation.

Domestic Violence and Animal Standpoint Theory

Loosely related to feminist standpoint theory, AST simultaneously acknowledges the emotional and embodied aspects of our relationships with animals and the need to include their perspectives rather than imposing our own upon them. At its most basic, it involves recognising the need to include animals in human thinking. As Josephine Donovan (2006, 306–7) puts it,

Feminists—indeed most women—are acutely aware of what it feels like to have one's opinion ignored, trivialized, rendered unimportant. Perhaps this experience has awakened their sensitivity to the fact that other marginalized groups—including animals—have trouble getting their viewpoints heard … Just, therefore, as feminism has called for incorporating the voices of women into public policy and ethical discourse, so feminist animal advocates must call for incorporating the voices of animals as well.… [This] means learning to see what human ideological constructions elide; to understand and comprehend what is not identified and recognized in these constructions; to, in short, attempt to reach out emotionally as well as intellectually to what is different from oneself rather than reshaping (in the case of animals) that difference to conform to one's own human-based preconceptions.

Beyond this, AST includes implicit recognition of power asymmetry between the species and seeks to rectify this—at least partially—by considering the crucial roles animals play in historical and contemporary societies.

Domestic violence is ultimately about the abuse of power but so often involves the manufacture of compliance to another's domination and coercion, until awareness of the gravity of the situation crystallises and escape/rescue is made possible. This holds for human and animal victims, including those left unaided for many years. Animals may need to be extremely subservient to the humans who abuse them or risk their lives. One of the aims of AST is to redefine "the dysfunctional power systems that structure our relationships to one another, to other species, and to the natural world, in hierarchical rather than complementary terms" (Best 2014, 1). In seeking to undermine speciesism, AST also aims to destabilise the mechanisms that maintain other forms of oppression—sexism, racism, and so on. Just as feminist standpoint theory seeks to validate oppressed women's understandings of the social world and various practices in it, AST recognises the intrinsic value of animals rather than simply arguing for recognition of their—always partial—extrinsic value. This has the added advantage of bringing all animals—not just companion species—into our thinking.

While plenty of critiques have been made about standpoint theory more generally (see, e.g., Harding 2004), we think the strength of AST in the current context is that it facilitates thought about how to include animals in domestic violence theory and service provision. And it does so in ways that disrupt, rather than reproduce, the hierarchical and binary thinking that underpins the violence done to victims, animals and humans. Incorporating ideas from AST has the potential to extend our theoretical understanding of the mechanisms of abuse and oppression, to include animals more fully. It can also inform our practice. For example, acknowledging that animals are caught up in domestic violence as victims in their own right opens the door to research to clarify precisely how they experience violence, how they try to recover from it, both similarly to, and differently from, humans. Among many others, some of the questions to consider include the following:

- How does the stress and trauma of violence affect animal companions in domestic settings, and how might we better be able to help them recover?
- How can animals' experience of domestic violence at the hands of one gender (such as men) lead to problems rehoming animals with that same gender in the future? Is this something we need to consider when relocating animals away from violence?
- How does being separated from human family members, and/or other animal family members, affect animals after witnessing domestic violence?
- What specialist intervention and recovery services might companion animals need to overcome physical and emotional trauma as a consequence of domestic violence?
- How might we better train those living and working with animals to address their needs relating to surviving domestic violence, to give them a better chance at recovery and future stability in housing?
- How might we train those in positions of authority, such as veterinarians, to address animal abuse in the context of domestic violence?
- What intervention and reporting strategies might work best for animal victims of domestic violence?

At the moment, these kinds of questions go largely unasked and unanswered. Speciesism has laid the foundations for the non-recognition of animal experience. Shifts to acknowledge companion animals as family members have occurred but even when this happens, the animals' experiences of violence are likely to be subsumed under that of their human family members. As a result, animal suffering may be extended and intensified, first through abuse and neglect and then if separated from their humans trying to escape violent homes. One way to begin to rectify this is to attempt to understand what animals' experiences of domestic violence and abuse are. In the next section we outline the—problematically sparse—research that has begun to consider the impact of domestic violence and abuse on other animals.

Impact of Domestic Violence on Animals

An important message of this book is that domestic violence affects companion animals, not just humans. It is a simple but important point to reiterate given the vast majority of work on links between domestic violence and animal abuse focuses on human victims, with animals framed as 'red flags' that indicate intervention is needed for humans. In earlier chapters we explained how domestic violence directed at animal companions usually occurs at the same time as human-human domestic violence, making it an important indicator of human-human domestic violence. If we accept the idea that animals have a right to live their lives without abuse and cruelty, then the acknowledgement of domestic violence done to animals must not simply occur to (1) prevent human-human violence or (2) help human victims recover. Recognition must be given to the potential terror of domestic violence, for *both* animals and humans. Admittedly, this is not so easy to do.

Few studies have considered the effects of domestic violence on animals directly. Despite early calls to acknowledge the emotional effects of experiencing/witnessing violence on animals (Vermeulen and Odendaal 1993), the little research that does exist in this area foregrounds the physical impacts. For instance, attention has been given to the abuse of dogs, followed by cats, and then other commonly kept domesticated species such as chickens, rabbits, and rodents (Grugan 2018; Tiplady et al. 2012, 2015; Tong 2016). Men appear to be the primary domestic abusers of animals (Grugan 2018) who are subject to a wide variety of deliberate physical abuses including kicking, punching and/or hitting, abusive holding (e.g., by ears, or hanging), throwing, forms of torture (e.g., mutilation and burning), and shooting (Grugan 2018; Williams et al. 2008; Tiplady et al. 2012).

The women we spoke to for the *Loving You* project confirmed the findings of other research when they told stories of their animals being kicked, punched, and thrown, often to coerce the women into compliance, including returning to their abusers. They told of the ways companion animals can be targeted by abusers, and/or used as proxies for controlling spouses and children. For instance, Linda reported that her abusive ex-husband deliberately killed their cats, in one instance in front of the children. Many of the women we talked to tried to figure out how best to protect themselves, their children, and their companion animals. For instance, Nolene recounted how she had to leave her cats with her abuser and how

> [t]hree days later my ex-partner found me at my parent's house. Stood out the front of my house, circling it with his mum, calling to my son, with my cat in his hand, by the throat and telling me that if I didn't take my son out and give my son over – he was bargaining my cat for my child, and ended up throwing my cat.

Similarly, in the LGBTQ and animals studies led by Damien Riggs (Riggs et al. 2017a, b, 2018), we saw constant references to the physical abuse of animals. For example, one respondent said, "she [ex-partner] kicked my dog and caused him to urinate" and how they were "worried about the dog." Further comments included "Abuse directed towards dog still features in my flashbacks."

Like humans, animals experience physical *and* emotional effects from direct or witnessed violence (Riggs et al. 2018). Little research has focused on emotional/psychological abuse of animals within domestically violent situations, but there is increasing recognition that it needs to be addressed, that the matter is serious and the potential consequences dire. For example, Williams et al. (2008) in their survey of New Zealand veterinarians found that 86 of their 373 (23%) respondents stated they had seen animals who they considered to have been deliberately psychologically abused. Again, dogs (92%) were the species reported by veterinarians in this sample as most likely to experience psychological abuse, followed by cats (29%), horses (17%), cattle (10%), birds (5%), goats (3%), and pigs (5%).

For some animals, just as with humans, part of surviving the emotional abuse involves a fatalistic acceptance of violence as a norm, something that they need to adapt to and change their behaviour to avoid. *Loving You* interviewee Katrina told us how Maddie, her dog, was

> so conditioned to it [domestic violence] that she thought she was engaging in play, you know what I mean? He [abusive ex-partner] was overly rough with … He wouldn't create injuries so to speak, but he was so, so rough and dominant. She had to cower down to him before she was allowed to come inside. And if we opened the door he'd be going like this at her [gestures the need for her to submit] and she'd cower down. Then it was 'you may enter my house'. She was forever walking around with her head down and her tail between her legs. She was so uncertain of herself.

As well as the immediate injuries animals can suffer as a result of domestic violence, there are longer-term emotional health issues that can manifest as stress-related illness. Maddie struggled for a long time with stress-related skin issues that became infected when she was left with her abuser until Katrina could find animal-friendly accommodation. Maddie's infection became so bad Katrina considered having to euthanise her. Katrina explained:

> I think we spent five weeks homeless, we were living in a motel with the three kids and I applied for everywhere with an animal. It was getting to a point where I was considering not being able to have her. I had no idea what I was going to do with her especially with her allergy condition because it's really hard to manage. By the time my friend had gotten her she was completely infected … it wasn't so much that she wasn't having her medication because there were people who were swearing black and blue we're giving her her medication. It was a stress response … she was so badly infected. I mean it was getting to a point where in my head I'm thinking we might even have to put her down. That was very much right at the back of my head and I was going to do everything possible to get a place [that allowed animals]. But the barriers that that creates are unbelievable. To have a pet on a private lease is crazy, especially in the rental market at the moment.

Katrina emphasised the gravity of the situation by indicating how she had wrestled with the idea of euthanising Maddie because of her skin condition and because she could not, at this point, find accommodation that allowed animals. With the odds against them, Katrina persevered largely because of her empathic connection with and love for Maddie. Fortunately, the Northern Domestic Violence Service, a pet-friendly women's shelter, came to the rescue. However, had this service not existed, the outcome for Maddie could have been dramatically different. In terms of service responses, we need to offer more than pot-luck to domestic violence survivors. Questions about housing and other material living conditions have added significance given the ongoing exposure to violence caused behavioural and emotional reactions in many of the animals that we met, and heard about, in our projects.

Most of the animals tried to convey their distress and unhappiness, as Jacqui explained about her dog Baz:

> And at first, I was a bit worried. I even took my dog, I was that worried that I took my dog down to best friend's place down at Morphettville and left him there for a couple of days. And because I just didn't know what the ex was going to do, and then the ex said to me that he wanted the dog back. And you know so I thought, "well, I'll see, if he can look after the dog then maybe we'll come back", you know. He looked after the dog but the dog just didn't want to be there. That's why he stopped eating and stuff like that, so I never forgave myself for leaving the dog, but you can't really take him to a hotel.

Stress-related responses from animals appear to be exacerbated by the usually forced separation they have to endure from their humans. 'Shared custody' arrangements can be problematic for animals after humans separate. One of the respondents to the LGBTQ and animal companions project explained, "On advice I agreed to 50:50 as temp arrangement to be reviewed. Every 2 weeks dog went back and forth between homes. She had to be medicated for anxiety and I had a near breakdown" (see Riggs et al. 2018). Similarly, *Loving You* interviewee Nadia explained how her cats, Tigger and Abbey, were affected by having to live with the constant threat of domestic violence, and how she didn't necessarily notice their behaviour changes fully until they all moved away from their abuser:

They [cats] would go and hide. We [her and ex-partner] had the front bed-room and they would go all the way down to the back, the lounge room at the back of the house and go behind the couch and hide in there. *Sounds weird but they were depressed* ... while he [abusive ex-partner] was at work and everything they'd just sit in the bedroom. We had the bed set up near the window and stuff and they'd just sleep all day and not do anything ... *that's not the cats I remember.* They're always following me around and doing stuff, Ellie the fluffy one loves playing and they, they would just sit in their beds and do nothing. And it was really, really horrible I think when I came here and they started to come back out of their shells. It made me really upset because I thought, *"Wow I didn't realise how down you guys were."*

Domestic violence, especially when it is chronic, can be demoralising if not depressing for all sentient beings who are likely to be met with differ-ent forms of abuse from their perpetrators, irrespective of whether they repress themselves or withdraw or act out (Fraser 1999; Taylor et al. 2017). The details of how this plays out for companion animals are largely unknown. The limited available research reveals stress- and anxiety-related behaviours (aggression, fleeing) are common outcomes of emo-tional abuse for animals (Tiplady et al. 2012), and these behaviours may well persist after the animal is no longer in the violent situation (Tiplady et al. 2015). The impact of violence can compromise both the animal's healing process and their chances of remaining with their human caretak-ers and/or chances of being rehomed (if necessary) if their behaviour becomes extremely problematic. Tiplady et al. (2015), for instance, docu-ment that while behavioural changes apparent in animals living in domes-tically violent households tend to become less severe after leaving the violence, some dogs exhibit a generalised fear of men that continues long after the end of the violent relationship. This can lead to negative conse-quences for the animals, as Tiplady et al. (2015, 132) explain:

There was an ongoing impact on the behaviour of animals which persisted after the exposure to the violence and abuse had ceased. Some of the observed behaviour changes included seeking proximity to the woman owner, indicating that the animal remained anxious, and, in some cases, animals demonstrating a fear of men which appeared to be generalised. Behavioural rehabilitation was provided to one animal (a dog), resulting in his being successfully rehomed. A fear of men may have implications for the animal's ability to settle into a foster home that includes men, to cope with male veterinary staff and animal attendants, or to feel comfortable with any male relatives, friends or future male intimate partners of the abused woman or her children. Overall, the current study showed that exposure to domestic violence can have ongoing impact on animals' emotions, especially an enhanced level of fear and anxiety. The ongoing difficulties that animals exhibited were either the result of being abused directly or being exposed to domestic violence. Animal abuse is a traumatic event causing fear and helplessness in animals and in many cases ongoing (longer than one month) behavioural changes.

Companion animals are usually reliant on humans to respond to their distress. McMillan et al. (2015) studied 69 dogs deemed by a diverse panel of experts to meet the criteria of likely to have been abused. Caregivers of the animals in question were asked to complete the C-BARQ (the Canine Behavioral Assessment and Research Questionnaire) and results were compared to a control group (of 5239 dogs). Results showed the abused dog group were more likely to have behavioural problems such as being more excitable and being prone to attachment/attention-seeking behaviour. Abused dogs were also more likely to show aggression and fear towards unfamiliar humans, dogs, and unusual places (e.g., stairs).

The dogs in the 'abused' cohort in McMillan et al.'s (2015) study, for example, showed higher (i.e., 'poorer' in behavioural terms) levels in 12 different characteristics measured, and 8 of these (including aggression and fear directed towards unfamiliar humans and dogs) are high on lists of reasons why people surrender their animals to shelters. New et al. (2000) collected data on 2631 dogs and puppies relinquished by 2092 people and 2374 cats and kittens relinquished by 1315 people in the US. They found that dogs at an increased risk of relinquishment were those who frequently soiled in the house, were considered overly active, or were considered fearful. Cats were at increased risk of relinquishment if they soiled the house, caused damage, or were considered overly active. Animals suffering through their own emotional trauma are thus at increased risk of surrender due to behavioural problems, as well as risk of being repeatedly homed and then returned to shelters due to their behaviour. This 'revolving door' in turn often leads to their behavioural problems being exacerbated (New et al. 2000).

As is the case for many humans, animals' simply leaving the violent situation is not enough to remedy any emotional or behavioural effects. Many of the companion animals we met continued to display signs of separation anxiety and other distress when their humans are away from them, and this appears to have been exacerbated by their initial separation at the time of the human fleeing domestic violence. Nolene explained:

[T]hat's the other thing that people sometimes don't appreciate is that the impact on the cats, the impacts on the animals, not just the domestic violence experience but just the separation.

Allison echoed this in relation to her dog, Freddy:

[I]t's just pure unconditional love … the only time he [Freddy the dog] was upset with me was the five weeks that we were separated before I came here. After that he started to get a bit better. The first night I was here with him I actually had to go out and I'd never heard him howl before…. When we first got here, he chewed up all of the front door he did a better job than white ants. And that would've taken him hours, and I would've loved to have a webcam just to see it…. And I came home, stayed for about an hour and then went out again. And a normal dog would be alright with that but *I have to be aware of the fact that he's been through just as much and he's still dealing with it too, I'm sure.*

Allison empathised with Freddy's trauma, but it took a bit of time. This is not surprising given the little public attention paid to animal companions' experiences of domestic violence and attempts at recovery. That she noticed it all and sought to respond more sensitively to his trauma is noteworthy.

It is also not surprising that animals who have experienced or witnessed domestic violence suffer from separation anxiety. In the clinical literature, canine separation anxiety is defined as an anxiety-related disorder as a result of "emotion of apprehension to an anticipated danger or threat" (Ogata 2016, 28–29). And while the idea of cats suffering from separation anxiety is more contentious, Schwartz (2002) found that some cats do develop it as evidenced by their displaying clinical signs, including destructive behaviour and household soiling. As Shreve and Udell (2015, 1200) note, "If cats can form an attachment bond with their owners, it may be expected they can experience separation anxiety."

Many of our respondents explicitly referenced anxiety when discussing their animals; for example, Allison told us how Freddy

> gets stupid when he gets really anxious, I can be away from him for 10 minutes or a day and a half and … he gets quite, he can't stop himself and so I taught my daughter, I'll be, "Go calm him down." Because he'll start doing a tail chase and he can't stop his back leg going and it's just for pure either excitement or just anxiety, so you just have to sit there and calm him down.

To compound the separation many animals suffer when their humans enter temporary accommodation while fleeing domestic violence, they may also be forced to spend long periods alone post-separation as their humans with precarious working situations need to work long hours to make financial ends meet. Brianna explained how her dog, Max,

> was on his own a lot. Yeah, I wish I could take him with me, but yeah that was making me sad. I was, 'Oh my God I have to leave him' … *he knew that*. I was really upset you know what I mean? He'd always be crying at the door if I didn't let him in straight away he'd be … then come and sit next to me so that might be why he's so cuddly now.

Brianna noticed Max's agency when she said that 'he knew' that she had to leave him. Like Katrina, who tried to respond more sensitively to her dog, Brianna connected Max's past experience of separation and abuse with him being 'so cuddly now.'

We also heard about other emotional/behavioural problems in animals during their post-violence recovery. For instance, previously non-violent animals would display aggressive behaviour, in keeping with what is known about trauma and separation anxiety in animals (Ogata 2016). Nadia told us about her cats being uneasy and violent when she came back to them after their initial separation. Importantly she explains how it took a lot of work with one of her cats, Abbey, to address that behaviour:

> [W]hen I actually got her back she was quite uneasy, very violent. She would attack me a lot and I thought, 'Well I'm definitely not going to get rid of her at all'. That was not a thought whatsoever. *I thought, 'No, I'm going to stick this out. Maybe she [Abbey the cat] just feels really uncomfortable with the situation being around violence and being moved from house to house?* And I don't think she was getting enough stimulation and love where she was. So, I stuck it out and yeah kept her, and made sure that I didn't get rid of her at all. [I] didn't have that thought in my head. I thought, 'No, be persistent'. And yeah here we are. *She's still with me and she's absolutely fantastic.*

The repetition in Nadia's story shows the extent of her dilemma when it came to persevering with Abbey, her cat, who was acting out from her own experiences of the domestic violence. Similar to many of the other women we interviewed, Nadia looked beyond the difficult behaviours the animals were exhibiting to understand why it was happening and what might need to be done about it.

Similarly, Lucy told us how Leo, her cat, who had not been abused directly still behaved differently as a result of witnessing her abuse and/or having to move as a result of the abuse.

> [He] weed on me to wake me up and that really made me angry.
> Q: That's weird isn't it? Has he ever done that before?
> A: No, never. I don't know if he was fretting, like whether it was like he was scared that he was here. Because he hadn't been outside before.

The negative impact on the animals is often exacerbated by the less-than-ideal situations they are often forced into while their human care-takers seek alternative accommodation. Allison explains how she had to leave her dog Freddy with someone who lived with another male dog who did not mix well with others. As a result, Freddy was left outside until Allison visited, and Allison herself had to act in less than ideal ways to facilitate this:

They couldn't be together because they were both prominent male species so the only time he would come in is when I was there. I'd get this girl [looking after Freddy] some weed [cannabis] or whatever, like that and give her money … sometimes I couldn't, could barely even afford to get back to the [very budget] hotel [where she was staying]. *But as long as he [Freddy] was okay, I was okay.*

The last line shows how Allison's sense of well-being is tied up with Freddy's. Sadly, Freddy's condition was not okay. Allison explained how Freddy didn't adapt well to his new surroundings, refusing to eat so that when they were reunited he was underweight. There were also other signs showing he hadn't been cared for properly:

He [Freddy] gets in the car and actually he's a ball of just firecracker he was. *He was so skinny* – And he, it'd obviously affected him and, and he had in total, *he had 5 grass seeds in his feet.*

Other women explained their families stepped in to house their animals while they were in temporary accommodation, usually motels. Nolene recounted how her cats, Harley and Sam,

had to live in a tiny room in my parents' house. They weren't okay with that. So, my parents had to eventually get a caravan and put them in the caravan, and that's where I lived. Of course, courts don't necessarily like people living in a caravan.

Nolene had the option of living in her parents' caravan with her child and cats. However, she was forced to decide against this because she knew that the family law court would think poorly of them living in a caravan, and she did not want to lose custody of her child.

While the people we have talked to for our various projects indicate having strong bonds with their animals, many were in untenable situations. These untenable situations could mean they had to put their own safety first, as well as that of their children. With few services available to help animals, animals are often left at the mercy of abusers and/or are sent into less-than-ideal circumstances with others who sometimes take on their care with reluctance. Katrina revealed how, despite loving her animal companions deeply, she fled without them and, at that point, without much concern for them:

> [T]o be honest I left on the drop of a hat. I wanted to be prepared. I wanted to have everything all my ducks in a row. But I left at the drop of a hat. It was a bag of clothes. *I didn't even give a second thought to my animals, to be honest.* I just got out of there. … Afterwards of course I stressed about Maddie because not that I thought he [abusive ex-partner] would hurt her, but her quality of life would've been really poor. I mean, you can see she's a baby, she needs attention. She needs affection.

Recognising Maddie's needs now, Katrina is to be respected for her honesty. Few people would be willing to admit they didn't give a second thought to their animals. An important benefit of her doing so is we can reflect on the level of danger posed to animal companions, remembering that most live their lives in human captivity.

Despite the lengths that many domestic violence victims/survivors go to, either take their animals with them or arrange alternate care for them, some animals have to be re-homed/surrendered. Belinda explained that while she managed to keep her dog, she had to rehome her cat "because there's no way I could have cats here." Brianna had to rehome her original dog, partly to protect him from the abuser and partly because of his aggression after suffering abuse:

> Yeah, he [abusive ex-partner] actually picked him [dog] up one day and dropped kicked him across the room. So – and that was it … Yeah, I had to get rid of him [dog] because of that—because of my ex being violent.

Brianna also explained how financially she struggled with her animals, and how she nearly got rid of her cat, "a few times because I was struggling to actually feed her."

We understand the reasons for human domestic violence victims/survivors' fleeing violence in their homes and, in the process, leaving animals with abusers. We appreciate the need for humans to temporarily accommodate animal companions in less-than-ideal situations or surrender them to animal rescue organisations. We know that when money is scarce, food for both humans and animals can be a serious problem. Most importantly we know that the responsibility for domestic violence, and its effects, must lie at the feet of those who perpetrate it, not just the cultural contexts that give rise to it, or the service gaps, limitations, and failures to adequately respond to it.

The idea that victims/survivors should be held accountable for the adequacy of the protection of other victims/survivors requires critical analysis (Carlton et al. 2013). This cultural expectation is unfair and unreasonable for two main reasons. The first is that most perpetrators of domestic violence are men (numerically and for serious injury or homicides) and often have most, if not total, control over the household's finances and often movements of family members. The second is that most victims/survivors likely to be held to account for others' protection from harm are women—the same people often still expected to perform the bulk of unpaid domestic and emotional labour in the family and may be financially, not just emotionally, dependent on the people who violate them.

If we are to make major advances in this area, we need to go beyond these constructed stereotypical poles of recognition/non-recognition, blame, shame, and responsibility. If there is blame to be had, then collectively we must share it. We need to acknowledge all the human actions, which, at least potentially, can place animals at great risk of harm. Beyond the humans who abuse them and/or frighten them with the abuse they perpetrate against others in the household, and beyond the victims who flee without them, we all share responsibility for the treatment of animals in our societies. This includes the humans who take on the temporary care of animals professing to help out only to ignore or neglect them, and policy and law makers and services that ignore the existence and relevance of animals. Dramatic change is needed to recognise the place of animals in domestic settings (as well as elsewhere) and make visible their needs, rights, and welfare.

As it used to be for children in situations of domestic violence (see Fraser 1999), animal companions might not be seen, noticed, or remembered (also see Riggs et al. 2018). In the confusion and crisis, there is a real risk that when humans step forward to help, it will be help offered to the humans in distress. Animal companions may be forgotten, ignored, or treated as an afterthought. Some come to the attention of humans through their 'bad behaviour.' As outlined earlier, when animals are exposed or subjected to domestic violence, behavioural problems are likely to result. These problems can negatively impact their ability to settle with their humans in the future. For animals who cannot accompany their humans and are forced into new homes, they must deal with the loss of their human/s with whom many will have had close relationships. As well as the emotional toll this can take, there is the risk of developing other behavioural problems, which can further threaten their ability to settle into new homes (Lepper et al. 2002).

That said, many animals and humans find their life, health, and well-being greatly improved after leaving abusers. Katrina told us how Maddie changed physiologically, in that her allergies cleared up, and behaviourally:

> I mean she's changed as a dog, she has changed; she's gone from this timid scared little puppy that would walk around with no confidence whatsoever and now she's the protector here…. If something made a noise she'd come and hide behind you like, 'protect me Mum, protect me'. Now she's the protector, she's the Mother; she goes [a]round, she cleans all the kids and they get home from school and they know, they just sit there. She'll just completely cover them in drool, but that's something she has to do to make herself feel – now she's free as well. *She's free and I can see it by her skin.* That's a half – I think I gave her, half a steroid. We were on two steroids a day. It was killing her; her life would've been halved and it effects every part of her system. It was killing her and now she's on a half.

Katrina's use of the phrase "we were on two steroids a day" speaks to the emotional closeness she felt towards Maddie during their joint recovery period. Her concern for Maddie's health is obvious, as the connection she makes between Maddie's skin and environmental stress levels.

Nadia explained how her cats, Abbey and Tigger, have also changed for the better since moving into their new home:

> It's been really nice to see the way they've bounced back, how frightened they were at the beginning. Someone would come because there was a couple of things needed to be done around the house when I first moved in. How frightened they were when people came to the door…. Just he was so frightened I remember putting them in the bathroom because

this guy had to come in and out of the house a lot. When I went to get them they were both curled up behind the toilet, the two of them together. There they were. They looked so scared and it just made me feel so horrible and so…. it feels nice seeing them back to themselves. Abbey, especially, just went from just not interacting much with me anymore and not to, she's become even more cuddly than she was before all this happened…. she loves playing, she, she's always been a cat that bats balls around and stuff but she didn't do that for a while. Even when I first moved here she didn't really do it much and then the last few weeks she's just gone nuts, running up and down the hall.

Nadia's observations show a deep engagement with her cats. She recognised the cats' reactions are directly linked to the domestic violence they were exposed to. Noticing Abbey's return to playing with balls was just one sign of her recovery.

One of the clear benefits of human-animal relationships during recovery from domestic violence is the sense of connection and the modelling of positive, close relationships (Riggs et al. 2018; Taylor et al. 2017). As Herman (2015, 133) points out, "The core experiences of psychological trauma are disempowerment and disconnection from others. Recovery, therefore, is based upon the empowerment of the survivor and the creation of new connections. Recovery can take place only within the contexts of relationships." The data we have from our various projects makes it clear that the empathic connections and love between humans and animals can help both heal from the trauma of violence. For example, when asked what Maddie means to her, Katrina responded,

She [Maddie the dog] means knowing what a healthy relationship is. *She's teaching me what a healthy relationship is based on mutual respect.* She knows my boundaries, I know her boundaries. There's unconditional love and that's something I think a lot of abused women don't understand is what real unconditional love is because there's … because there's always conditions when you're with an abuser. Everything's based on conditions and a lot of abused women are givers and this relationship gives back. I think that she's [Maddie] teaching me about, yeah, she's teaching me about life— about what life is supposed to be.

As is clear from the discussion above, animals are usually deeply affected by domestic violence. This needs to be recognised in current thinking about domestic violence both theoretically and in terms of service responses. We consider both these aspects in the remainder of this chapter.

Conceptualising Domestic Violence to Include Animals

Recent definitions of domestic violence have moved to include any 'incident' that involves violence. And while, superficially, this is to be welcomed as a potential way of marking the unacceptability of interpersonal violence, in actuality it leads to a skewed reading of the prevalence of domestic violence, which in turn has led to claims it occurs equally between men and women. As Kelly and Westmarland (2016) note, such an 'incidental' approach mirrors the language that men use about their violence intimating that it was a one-off event or occurrence. Doing so helps to minimise the impact and deny its effects.

Women's reports, however, still note the ongoing, repetitive, asymmetrical, and often terror-inducing patterns of domestic violence—abuse that paints a very different picture to domestic violence as separate and defined incidents (Johnson 2016). Early feminist understandings of domestic violence acknowledged this and were much more closely aligned with women's experiences than men's reports (see Dobash and Dobash 2003). These understandings were "theorised within the refuge movement and early research as an ongoing pattern of behaviour—not as one, two or three isolated 'incidents'. It is precisely the repetition, and the web of various forms of power and control used by perpetrators, that entraps women in abusive relationships" (Kelly and Westmarland 2016, 114). As Kelly and Westmarland point out, many of the coercive patterns of behaviour common to domestic violence would not be considered official 'incidents' (e.g., micro-managing appearances). This has relevance to the way we understand and theorise about how animal abuse fits into existing conceptualisations of domestic violence. In contrast to those that focus on 'incidents of abuse,' definitions of domestic violence that acknowledge its coercive aspects have room to include threats to, and actual harm of, companion animals. This is increasingly—and positively—being adopted, in terms of definitions of, and response to, domestic violence. For example, most jurisdictions in Australia now acknowledge that killing or injuring an animal constitutes domestic violence. Some acknowledge threats to harm or kill animals also constitute domestic violence (AVA n.d.). That is the good news. The not-so-good news is provisions for animals may only be extended to them based on their property status.

Assisting Animal Victims of Domestic Violence

In more recent years there has been an increased recognition of the links between human- and animal-directed violence, which has led to more community organisations offering help to humans fleeing domestic violence with their animals and—for mothers—their children. Some service responses have started primarily, if not exclusively, from the premise that they can help humans by helping their animals, that they can provide ways into populations sometimes classed as 'hard to reach.' Even so, this can provide momentum for a stronger recognition of animals as victims of domestic violence in the future. An injection of funding is needed, from government, non-government agencies, and business corporations, and the widespread regard for animal companions across these sectors might provide some impetus. Funding, infrastructure, and support are needed to build on the current offerings made at the local community level, often by resource-stretched agencies and unfunded volunteer groups, of whom at least some are staffed by working-class women living on low incomes.

Foster care may be offered for the animals while the women and children are in temporary accommodation, such as the services offered by *Safe Pets, Safe Families* in South Australia. As outlined above, these services are much needed, but it is imperative they are not driven primarily by human concerns. A partial, but not unproblematic, way of thinking about the kinds of services that might help animals is to ask their human caretakers who saw, first-hand, the effects of domestic violence on them.

We did this in the *Loving You, Loving Me* project and we conclude this chapter with a discussion of the suggestions for future action to help animals and their humans as they escape domestic violence together.

Some of the women we spoke to for the *Loving You* project had their own ideas about how to help animals and humans, including their children. As expected, many of these suggestions turned to ways to keep animals with their humans in initial temporary and later longer-term accommodation. The women made it clear they would not leave violent situations because of fear for their animals. As Nolene put it,

> What it [the domestic violence] is and location [housing]. They [this service] let you have the animals with you … So many people do not want to leave, because they can't – and the fear, the fear of is this animal going to be hurt [if they do].

Other recommendations concerned the financial feasibility of caring for animals who may have injuries and/or emotional problems requiring professional treatment. Nolene suggested that domestic violence services acknowledge this and help out, where possible, with the daily costs of living with an animal.

> Afterwards it's the practicality of being able to afford having your animal. That's another reason why people have to leave them, is, "I can't afford to look after myself, buy groceries, do a roof over my head and pay for the dogs." Dogs are expensive. The things that I think would be really good avenues is if a person has to leave and go into a shelter, that – and I've been considering this sort of stuff for quite a while, is support [for the animals]. Like, yes, there's food services for people, but how many of those actually have anything for pets, as in pet food, bedding for them as well? Because usually all that stuff has gone.

Nolene also suggested that the police, or other relevant officials, are given the right to enter people's property and remove the animal from a violent situation in order to reunite them with their owner. She explained that while the police will help ensure the safety of domestic violence victims by returning to their property to collect some of their belongings, there are no official avenues for returning to help secure the safety of animal companions. She noted that in the future, anyone given this right would need training in animal behaviour, to understand them including those that are aggressive. Another of Nolene's suggestion was to provide emotional support services to the animals who have experienced domestic violence, stating poignantly:

> [N]o one's thinking about the damn animals are they? That animal's there, been through a traumatic bloody experience, of seeing the person that they love get hurt, but there's no service for them. If *we're* suffering with stress, what about them?

Awareness training for professionals involved in domestic violence service provision was also recommended:

> I think they [professionals] really need not just head knowledge but a bit of open compassion to see exactly what these dogs or any dog or any animal does for a person who's been traumatised in such a way, where the deep healing of the scars need to mend. An animal can bring so much more than what they [professionals] see on the surface. *They [animals] can see the bruising, they can see the scars but [also] what's going on inside.* Yeah, she [human survivors of domestic violence] can get counselling but she can also get it by having a companion as such a dog or a cat.

We echo this but would also call for various other strategies to foreground the lived experience of animals. Conceptually, we need to extend the ways we think about domestic violence to include animals as victims as well as humans (see Chaps. 2 and 3). But we also need practical policies and provisions that embed a concern for animals' well-being in services, training, and domestic violence-related policy and processes. One of the many small steps that might be taken, for example, is to offer human domestic violence survivors information about the behavioural changes they might see in their animals, along with advice about how to cope with it and help their animal recover. Research by Blackwell et al. (2016) suggests such advice is readily taken up and can help animals settle following behavioural problems.

Our research suggests humans who have strong bonds with their animals empathise with them and are likely to be receptive to their needs, but there may also be critical lapses in the adequacy of their care, as we saw with Maddie the dog, among others. Working from the strength of these empathic connections is a positive and preventative way forward to provide and explain advice on domestic violence and animal-related care. We need to emphasise the patience and time needed to feel safe again and heal from traumatic past experiences, human and animal alike. It was a point noted by Linda that the recovery time for animals can be a long one and that their behaviour may be different after the abuse:

> It takes them a long time to get over it because you think about how we – it takes us such a long time. You think about the cat or the dog, how long it takes them because the trauma they've been through and just – you see how it cringes every time you – and you're not the perpetrator. But they're cringing in front of you…

Reflex cowering, or 'cringing' as Linda put it, is a common reaction to physical abuse, especially ambush attacks that occur without warning. The data we have from our various projects show many human survivors of domestic violence are acutely aware of the impacts of domestic violence on their animals, and it often gave them an additional sense of guilt from feelings they hadn't protected their animals sufficiently. Lucy said she recognised how deeply affected her two cats were even though they were not directly harmed by her abuser:

> Surely he [cat] was affected by it. He used to run away and stuff. He was only little too and he never got caught up in any of it [the violence]. He [abusive ex-partner] would smash glasses everywhere and [yet] he [the cat] never even got a piece of glass in his foot or anything. Because he would take off, obviously to protect himself. I don't know what he [the cat] thinks. Even my kids, when we're talking about pets, like it's – I don't know if it plays on his [the cat's] mind, if you know what I mean? … Like even if I get angry, he'll [cat] take off…. And even though he knows that I'm not going to hurt him … *he knows I'm not going to hurt him. I've never hurt him, but he still gets scared.*

Fear responses from domestic violence can be long-lived. Linda explained to us that she had seen the impact of trauma on the animals she lived with as a young person, the animals abused by her father. She made an instant connection between their trauma and hers:

> Far out. I've seen it. I've seen how it ... them and where you'd make big noise and it would start weeing itself. I'm thinking man just such trauma. I know how I used to feel when I was in a situation of being abused and that, and this poor little cat or dog any sound of a loud noise and then it'd shit itself. And the way it used to just run off and hide and [I'd] think, "Man – such defenceless little creature, and you've got this big human that's dumping all over it and treating it in such a disgraceful way." They didn't deserve – they didn't ask. It's like we don't be asked to be born into a certain family.

The trauma animals experienced was not linked solely to physical violence. Many animals were reported to have 'sensed' the violence coming. Brianna explains how her cat, Carla, would comfort her daughter whenever she started crying, which Brianna thought

> could have been because we were actually experiencing domestic violence at the time. Maybe Carla [the cat] actually sensed it, do you know what I mean? So, every time there was some sort of yelling or something she'd actually come up to us and check if we were okay. It was just amazing, I couldn't believe it, I'd never seen any animal do that before in my life and I thought, "Wow this cat's amazing, I'm so glad I got her."

Similarly, Brianna noted how her previous dog, who had experienced domestic violence with her, was in a constant state of vigilance, or hyper-vigilance, a symptom of PTSD and trauma in humans (Herman 2015):

> [H]e [dog] was actually quite protective of me, Teddy, and I don't know, there wasn't really much violence at that time. But I think he [the dog] could sense it, that he [abusive ex-partner] was that kind of person. Obviously, he'd been violent to Teddy so Teddy was always like ears pricked up [ready].

It needs to be noted that these reports of disturbances in animals' behaviours are coming from women who were not primed or actively supported to notice and puzzle through these changes. In the face of professional silence, many will turn to social media and the quality of advice they receive will vary. More research-based companion animal information is needed, along with service supports designed to manage the potential problems that might ensue not just from the violence but also if humans are not able to relocate with their animals. Some animals will be relinquished to shelters. Providing advice about animal surrender would also be useful.

Conclusion

We must recognise that some animals will not be better off remaining post-abuse with their human companions. While these instances appeared rarely in the various studies we have done, there were notable instances where the separation was warranted—for the animals' sake. For example, there were a couple of people who reported acting out against their animals, as a result of the violence done to them (the human). One respondent to the LGBT and animals research noted how "I was frightened and became angry at the animal for its behaviour, wishing if it understood to not poop/pee on the floor, then my ex-partners would not shout at it and scare it all the time", while another explained that their animals "[s]ometimes comforted me, other times I abused them too."

However, for many humans, shared experiences of abuse can lead to a stronger sense of empathy with their animals. One of the respondents to our LGBTQ and animal companions work told us how they "became closer to the animals [as] they seemed to empathise." Other people said it was the realisation of the effect of the abuse on animals that led to their decision to leave: "The impact on my dog was one of the final triggers for me leaving" (LGBTQ and animal companion respondent, 2016). What we don't know is if this increased connection routinely occurs for animals—do they become more attached to their humans as a result of co-suffering? Again, more research on the impact of domestic violence on animals is needed. Other species also need to be considered, particularly larger, and thus more difficult to accommodate, species. The majority of literature on the emotional impacts of violence on animals is both scarce and skewed towards dogs. Given the range of animals that live as companions with humans, and the risk that domestic violence poses to them, research on the impacts of domestic violence on other species is warranted. The fact remains that we simply do not know enough about the impacts of domestic violence on animals, as direct targets and as witnesses. Much more research is needed in this area in order to develop appropriate intervention strategies for animals, as well as develop post-trauma care processes and policies.

References

AVA, Australian Veterinary Association. (n.d.). *Family violence and the family pet.* Retrieved September 4, 2018, from https://www.ava.com.au/13451

Best, S. (2014). *The politics of total liberation: Revolution for the 21st century.* New York: Palgrave Macmillan.

Blackwell, E., Casey, R., & Bradshaw, J. (2016). Efficacy of written behavioral advice for separation-related behavior problems in dogs newly adopted from a rehoming center. *Journal of Veterinary Behavior: Clinical Applications and Research, 12,* 13–19.

Carlton, R. R., Krane, J., Lapierre, S., Richardson, C. L., & Strega, S. (Eds.). (2013). *Failure to protect: Moving beyond gendered responses.* New Brunswick: Fernwood Publishing.

Dobash, R. E., & Dobash, R. P. (2003). *Women, violence and social change.* London: Routledge.

Donovan, J. (2006). Feminism and the treatment of animals: From care to dialogue. *Signs, 31*(2), 305–329.

Fraser, H. (1999). Considering the needs of children exposed to domestic violence; a feminist perspective for practitioners. *Women Against Violence, An Australian Feminist Journal, 6,* 34–40.

Grugan, S. T. (2018). The companions we keep: A situational analysis and proposed typology of companion animal cruelty offenses. *Deviant Behavior, 39*(9), 1153–1169.

Harding, S. G. (Ed.). (2004). *The feminist standpoint theory reader: Intellectual and political controversies.* London: Psychology Press.

Herman, J. L. (2015). *Trauma and recovery: The aftermath of violence – From domestic abuse to political terror*. New York: Hachette.

Johnson, M. P. (2016). Conflict and control: Symmetry and asymmetry in domestic violence. In A. Booth, A. C. Crouter, M. L. Clements, & T. Boone-Holladay (Eds.), *Couples in conflict* (pp. 125–134). Hillsdale: Routledge.

Kelly, L., & Westmarland, N. (2016). Naming and defining 'domestic violence': Lessons from research with violent men. *Feminist Review, 112*(1), 113–127.

Lepper, M., Kass, P., & Hart, L. (2002). Prediction of adoption versus euthanasia among dogs and cats in a California animal shelter. *Journal of Applied Animal Welfare Science, 5*(1), 29–42.

McMillan, F., Duffy, D., Zawistowski, S., & Serpell, J. (2015). Behavioral and psychological characteristics of canine victims of abuse. *Journal of Applied Animal Welfare Science, 18*(1), 92–111.

New, J., Jr., Salman, M., King, M., Scarlett, J., Kass, P., & Hutchison, J. (2000). Characteristics of shelter-relinquished animals and their owners compared with animals and their owners in U.S. pet-owning households. *Journal of Applied Animal Welfare Science, 3*(3), 179–201.

Ogata, N. (2016). Separation anxiety in dogs: What progress has been made in our understanding of the most common behavioral problems in dogs. *Journal of Veterinary Behavior: Clinical Applications and Research, 16*, 28–35.

Riggs, D. W., Due, C., & Taylor, N. (2017a). 'I want to bring him from the aeroplane to here': The meaning of animals to children of refugee or migrant backgrounds resettled in Australia. *Children & Society, 31*(3), 219–230.

Riggs, D. W., Fraser, H., Taylor, N., Signal, T., & Donovan, C. (2017b). People of diverse genders and/or sexualities and their animal companions: Experiences of family violence in a bi-national sample. *Journal of Family Issues*, online first, https://doi.org/10.1177/0886260518771681

Riggs, D. W., Taylor, N., Fraser, H., Donovan, C., & Signal, T. (2018). The link between domestic violence and abuse and animal cruelty in the intimate relationships of people of diverse genders and/or sexualities: A binational study. *Journal of Interpersonal Violence*, online first, https://doi.org/10.1177/0886260518771681

Schwartz, S. (2002). Separation anxiety syndrome in cats: 136 cases (1991–2000). *Journal of the American Veterinary Medical Association, 220*(7), 1028–1033.

Shreve, K., & Udell, M. (2015). What's inside your cat's head? A review of cat (Felis silvestris catus) cognition research past, present and future. *Animal Cognition, 18*, 1195–1201.

Taylor, N., Fraser, H., & Riggs, D. W. (2017). Domestic violence and companion animals in the context of LGBT people's relationships. *Sexualities*, online first, https://doi.org/10.1177/1363460716681476

Tiplady, C., Walsh, D., & Phillips, C. (2012). Intimate partner violence and companion animal welfare. *Australian Veterinary Journal, 90*(1–2), 48–53.

Tiplady, C., Walsh, D., & Phillips, C. (2015). The ongoing impact of domestic violence on animal welfare. *Animal Studies Journal, 4*(2), 116–139. Retrieved August 13, 2018, from http://ro.uow.edu.au/asj/vol4/iss2/6

Tong, L. (2016). Identifying non-accidental injury cases in veterinary practice. *In Practice, 38*, 59–68.

Vermeulen, H., & Odendaal, J. S. J. (1993). Proposed typology of companion animal abuse. *Anthrozoös, 6*(4), 248–257.

Williams, V., Dale, A., Clarke, N., & Garrett, N. (2008). Animal abuse and family violence: Survey on the recognition of animal abuse by veterinarians in New Zealand and their understanding of the correlation between animal abuse and human violence. *New Zealand Veterinary Journal, 56*, 21–28.

Fig. 6.1 Woman hugging dog

6

Supporting Victims/Survivors: Escape, Refuge, and Recovery

Introduction

Throughout this book we have argued for the inclusion of non-human animals in the framing of domestic violence—as victims in their own right, with feelings, needs, and preferences—not just as red alerts to the harms experienced to and from humans. In Chap. 3 we discussed how to make companion animals more visible in our conceptualisation of domestic violence. To ground this discussion and provide more embodied and in-action portraits of lived experience, Chaps. 4, 5, and 6 include research participants' stories about living with companion animals and experiencing domestic violence together. Viewing their stories through the notion of empathic alliances and love, we witnessed how human-animal companionship can protect both parties' health and well-being but also make them vulnerable to each other's pain, hardship and fear of further mistreatment (also see O'Haire 2012). In Chap. 4 we also noted how shame, social stigma, internalised responsibility for an abuser's actions, and structural barriers such as (lack of) existence of relevant services, eligibility criteria, and distance to services are some of the possible complicating factors obstructing a victim's ability to declare

© The Author(s) 2019
N. Taylor, H. Fraser, *Companion Animals and Domestic Violence*, Palgrave Studies in Animals and Social Problems, https://doi.org/10.1007/978-3-030-04125-0_6

a relationship abusive and seek help (also see Crisafi and Jasinski 2016; Evans and Feder 2016). Most important to this book, we documented the already well-established factor preventing many victims/survivors of domestic violence from seeking help, and that is their (understandable) unwillingness to leave violent homes if it meant leaving companion animals with perpetrators (Ascione et al. 2007; Volant et al. 2008; Wuerch et al. 2017). It is a point that will be reiterated and expanded in this chapter through some of the stories told by the *Loving You* participants.

In Chap. 5 we foregrounded animals' experiences of domestic violence, to show how they can be affected in the short and longer term. We showed how companion animals can be caught up in webs of danger. Unlike human victims, particularly adults, they have no helplines to call and may not have others to notice their distress. If and when the time comes for human victims to depart, there is the heightened risk that they will be left behind to bear the wrath of the remaining abusive family members, abandoned entirely, or surrendered to an animal shelter where their lives may be at stake if no other humans who cross their paths decide they are worth taking home. No wonder so many of the animals display highly nervous, hyper-vigilant, and, at times, seemingly incomprehensible behaviours as a result (Tiplady et al. 2015). In this chapter we also note how vulnerable they are to being left with abusers, or taken with human victims fleeing abusers but hidden in accommodation (such as motels) that explicitly prohibit the entry of animals. We also notice how, during crisis periods, the animals may be cared for by humans who may be reluctant or resentful about providing such care. Still other risks involve them being surrendered to animal shelters, where they risk euthanasia if not rehoused.

Rethinking Escape

It is tempting to think that once victims of domestic violence flee their homes, they will be free to live their lives without violence. Tapping into dominant and longstanding narratives about rescue and escape, there is the common idea of escaping violence once and for all. It underpins the question, 'Why does she stay?'—a question that has historically portrayed women as either helpless through constructions of learned helplessness or hostage syndrome; or masochistic for staying (they must enjoy it, be used to it, and/or know no better) (Fraser 2005). These simplistic beliefs about escaping the violence once and for all are seductive and have surprising currency in mainstream Australia (Fraser 2005; Murray 2008) and internationally (Berns 2017; Rhodes and McKenzie 1998; Yamawaki et al. 2012). The stark reality for so many victims of domestic violence—human and animal—is a far cry from this (see García-Moreno et al. 2005; Herman 2015), unfairly shifting responsibility to victims to find ways to end the violence (Berns 2017; Harne and Radford 2008). Such beliefs inaccurately assume that victims will be safe if only they'd 'just leave' (also see Anderson et al. 2003; Murray 2008). These beliefs are misguided because they are built on the false dichotomy of being 'in' or 'out of' violence, when there is significant international evidence that the process of victims leaving their homes and setting up new lives can be fraught with serious danger (García-Moreno et al. 2005).

As we will show through our analysis of excerpts from *Loving You* participants' transcripts, there are several dangers to be traversed. For many victims there are dangers associated with anonymously getting information about domestic violence and possible support services and housing alternatives, let alone disclosing the abuse to others. Taking steps to get a service referral, departing the house and then setting up home somewhere else can all entail risks of retribution through escalated violence from perpetrators (also see Baker et al. 2010). We should not forget that post-separation is the time victims are more likely to be terrorised and (in some instances) killed (also see Johnson 2010). Old-fashioned patriarchal views, that is, a belief in the 'law of the father,' can merge with more contemporary expressions of hegemonic masculinity to form a cocktail of justifications for brutalising (heterosexual) women seen to have the audacity to leave 'their men' (see Johnson 2010; Harne and Radford 2008). Crudely put, it is the belief that heterosexual relationships begin and end when men say so, and only then. Vandello and Cohen (2003, 998) talk about this in terms of male honour and the conventions of feminine fidelity noting that

[b]ecause male honor often requires female deference and fidelity, relationships between men and women can carry an underlying tension that can serve as a precursor or catalyst to domestic violence. Honor may be used as a justification (either implicit or explicit) for violence; in the most extreme cases, it is used as a justification for homicides of spouses or family members in honor cultures.

Nolene, a woman from the *Loving You* project, described how her mother-in-law threatened her if she dared to leave:

> She [mother-in-law] went, "If you leave we will hunt you."
> Q: Is that what she said?
> A: That's what she said, "We will hunt you and we will take your son and you will never see him again."

Nolene's story shows not just how frightening it can be to try to leave a violent spouse but also the ways in which family members can conspire together to become a more formidable abusive force. Mother-in-law abuse has drawn attention internationally. For instance, abuse by mothers-in-law was the subject of a study by Roomani et al. (2016), who interviewed ten married heterosexual women in Pakistan subjected to domestic violence while living in their in-laws' home. They found that while women relatives (sisters-in-law, cousins) can participate in the abuse of other women, it is mothers-in-law who were most likely to abuse their daughters-in-law, and for two patriarchal reasons: failing to produce a son and/or failure to complete domestic duties up to the mother-in-law's standard (Roomani et al. 2016). In Nolene's case, the mother-in-law threatened to separate Nolene permanently from her young son if she fled the violence.

An Impossible Choice

Deciding to leave a family home because of domestic violence can be a major and very difficult decision (Anderson et al. 2003; Cameron 2015; Murray 2002, 2008). While the pressure may be on victims to suddenly flee their homes, there are often many complications that must be considered (Fraser 2005; Murray 2008). For many victims of domestic violence (especially those likely to become clients of public welfare, health, and education agencies), material practicalities are important considerations, such as income, housing, safety, and transport. These sit alongside the psychological difficulties faced (Yamawaki et al. 2012). At a time when they may be flooded with adrenaline and anxiety, victims usually need to problem-solve multiple issues: if they plan to leave, when and how will they get away? Do they have a car? Are they in a state to drive? Do they have any of their own money? Is there adequate security in the new place? If they are mothers, is the space suitable for children? If they live with animal companions, is there permission for them to live there too (also see Wuerch et al. 2017)? Will they all be safe at the new place? Is it affordable? Are supports available, and what is the access to transport and other amenities?

In the excerpt below, *Loving You* participant Nadia described how she secretly acquired information about domestic violence through her mobile phone and used it to assess whether her situation qualified as abuse:

> ...reading about abuse and stuff, when he'd go to work I'd read on my phone, I'd look at all these websites and stuff and I did these checklists, are you in an abusive relationship? And when you realise what's happening and you see the pattern and you see that that pattern is actually happening to you, the fact that harming pets is commonly on these lists, that really worried me because so far, he had followed all these steps. He'd isolated me from my family and friends. He did belittle me and he, he did make me feel like my reality wasn't real. He did all of those things.

Nadia noted that 'harming pets is commonly on these lists' of indicators for domestic violence. This kind of information is through various groups and their websites, such as *The Links Group* (UK) and the National Link Coalition (also see Lockwood and Arkow 2016).

As important as this information about the link was for Nadia to obtain, she now felt torn as she thought about possible places she could run to, including places that would not accept her cats. A lot of people are afraid to leave because as Nadia said, "Where am I going to go? What services can actually take me with my animals?"

The support the cats gave to her a few years ago and their involvement in her life as family made it unthinkable for Nadia to leave the house without them:

> I just feel like I'm responsible for these 2 little lives, so I can't just leave them, I can't give them to someone else to look after. I remember I was going through a really rough time a few years ago and the only thing that kept me going was the fact that, I have 2 lives that depend on me so... They are my family, my little family.

Nadia was not alone. All nine *Loving You* participants emphasised that housing was a major factor related to whether they felt able to leave; then, if and when they did leave, housing directly affected their overall experiences of health and well-being (also see Murray 2008). Like Nadia, Nolene also felt deeply connected to her cats. Yet, in the absence of pet-friendly accommodation, she fled without them:

> So, I had to leave – my cats were in the house … I had to leave … I got, under police protection. They took me to my parents, which is a while away … 3 days later my ex-partner found me at my parent's house. Stood out the front of my house, circling it with his mum, calling to my son, with my cat in his hand, by the throat and telling me that if I didn't take my son out and give my son over – he was bargaining my cat for my child, and ended up throwing my cat … Oh I remember it, I remember – I remember it way too well, so does my [5 year old] son.

Nolene repeated the phrase "I remember" three times to emphasise how etched this traumatic memory is in her and her son's minds. The trauma for both cats should also be remembered—one being thrown from the car and the other one making its own escape. The good news is that the cats remained with Nolene from that point onwards.

Help Can Be Elusive

People unacquainted with the complexities of surviving domestic violence may not realise that help can be elusive, even if the problem is known to others. For instance, in a New Zealand-based domestic violence and help-seeking study, Fanslow and Robinson (2010) found that more than 75% of their 956 respondents had reported the abuse to others and that of this group 40% reported that nobody helped them. So, rather than the violence being a well-hidden secret, it was known by others who provided little or no help or help that victims/survivors did not find to be useful (Fanslow and Robinson 2010). The title of a study investigating 16 British women's experiences of help-seeking during domestic violence makes this point: 'I could have just done with a little more help.' Notably, all 16 women in this study reported difficulties accessing help (Peckover 2003). This includes informal support from parents, siblings, friends, workmates, and neighbours, who may not offer the kind of support desperately needed. *Loving You* participant Nadia drew our attention to this issue. She spoke of her disappointment at the responses her mother and father made to her after separately asking for their help. She explained that her parents had separated when she was 12, due to domestic violence, and that she felt mostly ignored by them in the process. She had hoped that their knowledge of this would have motivated them to be more supportive of her now as an adult in need. But she found both parents dismissive. For instance, rather than offering her and her cats a place to stay, even in the short term, she said that her father reportedly complained that she'd "picked a bad week" to disclose the violence she was suffering, to which she responded bitterly, "Oh I'm sorry that leaving my violent situation is so inconvenient for you."

When help is needed for domestic violence but is not available from informal sources, formal support services can become ever more critical (Anderson et al. 2003; Victorian Government 2016). Yet, several barriers can get in the way of domestic violence victims reaching out to formal service providers (Evans and Feder 2016; Victorian Government 2016). From 485 victim surveys completed for their Ohio study, Anderson et al. (2003) found that almost half of all victims indicated returning to violent partners because of lack of money; more than a quarter because they did not have alternative accommodation; and one eighth (54 from 485) because they could not get help from the police. Focusing on domestic violence service provision in rural New South Wales in Australia, Owen and Carrington (2015) interviewed 49 rural service providers working in human services and the criminal justice system. They found that (heterosexual) women's attempts to obtain help was complicated by not just by the silence and shame surrounding domestic violence but also the women's economic dependency on men (also see García-Moreno et al. 2005). Being economically dependent on abusers certainly constrains options to purchase private goods and services without the permission of others, such as transport and alternative accommodation.

Help-seeking for domestic violence ordinarily requires the exposure of personal details, including those relating to past hardship and trauma, all of which can be hard to talk about (Rose et al. 2011). As discussed in Chap. 4, victim-blaming processes—intended and unintended—mean ultimate responsibility for responding to the violence is placed on the victim rather than the perpetrator. Fears of being victim-blamed by service providers may stem from negative past experiences with professionals, including the scrutiny of child custody arrangements if domestic violence in the home is admitted to (also see Holt 2016). 'Refusing to get (or accept) help' may also be used against victims, who delay seeking assistance, rendering them as irresponsible or complicit with the violence, especially if they are parents (Holt 2016). As Fugate et al. (2005) found in their Chicago-based study, victims of domestic violence who did not seek help from formal support services avoided doing so because they assumed they would be expected, if not directed, to leave their (abusive) spouses. It is well known that many victims want the violence, not their relationships, to end. For many heterosexual women abused by spouses, it is only when all hope is gone that final separation will be possible (Fraser 2005, 2008).

Sometimes the decision to leave a violent partner is planned in advance, while at other times it is made suddenly. In the excerpts below, Jacqui recounted how, on her 40th birthday, she made the decision:

The day that it happened it was … I was turning 40 … And it started off first thing in the morning where he got what he wanted.

Q: Sexually?
A: Yeah, [immediately after sex he] rolled over and I'm thinking, "Thanks, that was really good for me – not…" And then he started arguing with me in the bed and telling me, and bossing me around about what he wanted to do, and I thought, "Gee that's great." And

so basically, he turned around and said to me that he was going to take his son down to the athletics club, and [that] I would take the daughter and go and do the food shopping. I went "Okay." So, I did. I was shopping around and he called and I said "Oh, I'm here still going [but] I'm just about finished," which I was. And then of course I hit the checkouts at the worst time. Took me an hour to get through it. And then on the way home I forgot the milk. So, I've gone to the deli on the way and grabbed the milk, [I've] got home, he's out the front with his phone in his hand abusing the F out of me, saying that he was going to call the police because he called me 18 times or something. I didn't answer his phone calls because I knew he was just going to go off, so there's no point you know ...

Q: What, [all this] simply because you were late from food shopping?

A: Yeah ... Because I didn't answer the phone ... So basically while I unloaded the shopping, he was going around the house in front of the kids kicking objects, swearing at me. And I just put the shopping down and I walked up to him and I said "If you want to hit me now just do it, hit me because I've had enough," I said "I can't take it anymore." And he threw something at the ground and he went off. [Shortly afterwards] he turned around and he said that "I would rather you not be here, I would rather it be that I had the kids and you were dead", and that was it. And I said to myself, "Do you want to live with someone who wants you dead?" He wanted me to kill myself.

Domestic violence victims' susceptibility to attempting suicide was noted by British researchers Harne and Radford (2008, 40) who explained that "suicide and suicide attempts are usually carried out when women are so entrapped in relationships as a result of the coercive control carried out by perpetrators that they feel the only control left to them is to take their own lives".

Jacqui's story shows evidence of her partner's coercive control. It was her birthday, which in mainstream Australia means being treated with special privileges. Instead her day started with a sexual encounter that abruptly ends after her partner is satisfied. She is then instructed to go grocery shopping with their daughter, while he takes their son to the athletics club. We are reiterating this because such a delineation of roles and gendered use of time is part of a wider dynamic of patriarchal power and control that can be used to justify violence. One supposedly innocent way it does this is by relegating women and girls to activities that service the home, while boys and men are able to enjoy leisure time together. Quietly resentful, Jacqui and their daughter followed his instructions. But it was not enough to prevent an explosion. Arriving home later than expected and after refusing his 18 phone calls, Jacqui is subjected to a barrage of abuse by her (ex-)partner, who reportedly goads her into suicide. Her response is to retreat to the bedroom to self-medicate with codeine:

> And then I went into my room and I just stayed there, which is what I do, I would retreat into my bedroom and hide … He would leave me in the room, and I would, the majority of the time cry or I would go and get some codeine tablets. [Then] I went into my daughter's room. I laid on the bed and cuddled her, and then he came in again and abused the crap out of me in front of her, saying "Your mum's an f'in bitch", all this stuff. And that was it, that was enough for me to, because he went at her.

However, on this day things were different. Without money or a place to go, Jacqui did not acquiesce to her partner's demands this time but instead made the decision to leave him. The tipping point was him abusing their daughter:

> So, I went out to the car and I called the helpline. They said "I want you to get in the car, is there anywhere you could go?" I said "I could", but in the condition that I was in, and the distance …

> Q: Because you'd taken the codeine as well?
> A: Yeah and because I'm not very close to my parents…driving a long distance would not be a good idea. And she [support worker] said "Alright we'll get a motel for you, just drive to the corner of your street and stay there until we arrive", you know…. And I got out of the car and started packing up stuff and I said "I'm going to my mum's," he goes "Well if you're going to there you can take the kids." [Relieved] I went "Okay." So, then I grabbed a bag each … suitcase and grabbed whatever I could. It was all clothes, nothing else, because we just didn't have time. As I'd started up the car he'd slammed the door with the kids sitting on the front porch … so they came with me and then we went to the motel.

The worker on the helpline assisted Jacqui to escape the family home without endangering herself and her children by driving in a distressed state and under the influence of codeine. Instead of judging Jacqui for her codeine use, the worker organised a safer place for her and the children to stay. It was a motel paid for by a local domestic violence service, funded through state government grants.

Living from Day to Day in a Motel

In Australia, motels are mostly three-star-rated forms of accommodation that are generally clean, neat, and tidy. As social and community housing has been de-prioritised and with private housing markets now viewed as the best way to respond to housing demand, motels have been increasingly used to manage the risk of families, particularly families with young children, sleeping rough in their cars or on the streets. To the uninitiated, motel living might sound pleasant, even luxurious. The reality is that most motels are comprised of small rooms with combined sleeping and living quarters and, in some cases, a small kitchenette, adjoining an open, public car park. A few have pools and grassed areas but most do not. Unlike the US, where pet-friendly hotels are common, very few Australian motels allow pets. Many are located on busy roads and highways, providing less than ideal protection from the public gaze. For victims with children and companion animals, these quarters are not just likely to be cramped but also run the risk of perpetrators discovering their locations. Finding ways to distract children from the misery so often produced by violence is another challenge, as indicated by another excerpt from Jacqui (below):

Q: How long were you in the motel for?
A: March, April, May
Q: Oh god, that long?
A: Yeah living day by day … horrible … I went through a lot when I was in there because like we tried the reconciliation, I would go to things, but he just did his old [behaviours] …, He'd take the boy and off he'd go, so we might as well have not been together. And when I didn't do something that he liked, I got massive abuse for it again, so nothing ever changed.

Jacqui's reference to 'living day to day' relates to the need for victims/survivors to get daily authorisation of payment for the motel from their domestic violence service. This means that every morning they must be prepared to leave, in case permission is denied, making it anything but a relaxing holiday.

Informal supports from family and friends may provide viable alternatives to motel living but are not always available. Rhodes and McKenzie (1998, 398) remind us, "[W]e must not treat the issue of why battered women stay with their partners as if they (the women) exist in a vacuum. There are many sources of influence which can help or hinder a woman." In Jacqui's case (above), it was the distance between her and her parents, not just her use of codeine that prevented her driving to them. In Stella's case (below), it was past family conflict that restricted her being able to stay at her mother's house:

> My mum's just up the road but she can't – she won't have me there because my brother's there just because he has a problem with me about an incident and it's just yeah.

Q: There's bad blood there?
A: Yeah, but I'm hoping that'll change …

Recovery Over the Longer Term

Trying to recover from domestic violence, particularly chronic and severe forms, usually requires much support over the longer term, not just during the immediate separation phase (Richardson 2016; Victorian Government 2016). All nine women we interviewed for the *Loving You* project indicated needing support over the longer term, with some still having regular contact with their support workers up to three years post-separation. We are emphasising this point because, in these neoliberal times of welfare rationing and fast-paced, brief, and solution-focused interventions, it may be tempting to think otherwise. Similarly, we need to remember that addressing the multiple causes of domestic violence requires social and cultural transformation, not just remedial services for individual victims. It is a point made by Murray (2002), who while focusing on a Western Australian women's refuge, examined the changing responses to domestic violence since the 1970s. As she argued, since domestic violence takes hold within asymmetrical power relationships, responses made to eliminate it require much more than the provision of refuge (Murray 2002; also see Theobald et al. 2017).

In earlier chapters we reiterated the need to understand domestic violence as inclusive of a wide range of forms of abuse, including those that are psychological, sexual, financial, and physical (also see Rhodes and McKenzie 1998; Victorian Government 2016). Katrina told us that the abuse she suffered from her ex-partner went 'under the radar' because it did not involve physical assaults and how her husband maligned her in town and said she fabricated stories about him.

Q: Did they [people in the small town within which she was living] know how he was abusive to you?
A: No, everybody was very, *very* surprised.
Q: Were they.
A: *Very surprised* and I think it left it open for him to manipulate the situation more because the second I left that was it, there were stories left right and centre about how I was, you know how they turn everything over and attack your own personality, well that's exactly what he did.
Q: It was all your fault?
A: Yeah, all my fault. I'm an alcoholic [allegedly] yet I don't even drink. I've done this and I've done that. So, that [being publicly maligned and discredited by ex-partner] was more of a shock to me because I wasn't aware that that's what was going to happen.
Q: Has that made it difficult for you to go visit people back in the town?
A: Oh absolutely, well I work there as well.

Katrina stressed that emotional and financial abuse can be as negatively impactful as physical violence. Her story also shows that it can be hard/er to get help when (violent) partners are respected, if not loved, members of their communities. Post-separation and with the small-town rumour mills discrediting her (not just him), she had to find a way to keep her equanimity and her job, as she crafted a new life without him. The support she received from her domestic violence worker throughout this process helped her to do so (also see Evans and Feder 2016). This includes being given concrete information about what domestic violence can look like.

One of the many concrete examples of lists of behaviours used to classify domestic violence is the Artemis Intake Questionnaire, with 64 behaviours identified (Strauchler et al. 2004, 350). Here is a selection of them:

> 4. Threatened to abuse my pets.
> 5. Abused my pets.
> 6. Threatened to abuse my children.
> 7. Abused my children…
> 17. Controlled all the money…
> 25. Blamed me for the abuse.
> 26. Tried to control who I talked to or saw…
> 36. Told me he/she would find me and kill me if I ever left him/her.
> 42. Punched or kicked me.
> 43. Choked me.
> 44. Hit me with an object.
> 45. Was violent to me in front of the children…
> 62. Came home unexpectedly to check on me.
> 63. Would not let me use the phone…

To the outsider, these items might appear self-evidently abusive. For some victims/survivors, especially those who have been chronically discredited and maligned, it can be shocking, challenging, and distressing to find these descriptors relevant to their situations.

Parenting Challenges Post-Separation

Challenges to parenting may also emerge post-separation. Parents escaping domestic violence are charged with the responsibilities of managing the likely effects domestic violence exposure can have on their children (see Fraser 1999; Victorian Government 2016). Holt's (2016) Irish study of heterosexual women's experiences of abusive men post-separation showed how, if they come to the attention of child protection authorities because of domestic violence, they are likely to be assessed through a deficit model of mothering. She showed how, paradoxically, women's attempts to protect their children from fathers' abuse post-separation can result in them being charged (informally or formally) with interfering with men's right to have ongoing contact with their children (Holt 2016). Additionally, young people's pain, anger, fear, and resentment can erupt post-separation and may be directed at the non-abusive parent and others (also see Fraser 1999). Problems may stem from a sudden change in place of residence but also if there is instability in housing tenure (also see Baker et al. 2010). Based in the UK and focusing on bed and breakfast accommodations, Bowyer et al. (2015) discussed how difficult it can be for children exposed to domestic violence to move into temporary accommodation, how they may have little control over the decision to move. Focusing on girls aged 10–16 years, they found the girls commonly reported finding it difficult to process their experiences of violence when their living situations remained insecure and unstable (Bowyer et al. 2015). Jacqui provided an example of this when she described needing to manage her daughter's refusal to trust others after they separated, and her daughter's abusive behaviour:

> She [young daughter] won't go to any male doctors, she won't go near anyone, I have a real problem with her…even [with] my grandma and grandpa. It just depends on what day [whether] she decides to be good to them. [Otherwise] she's really rude, she's really nasty. Yet, she's a beautiful little girl.

> Q: She's working some stuff out?
> A: The abuse I used to get from him, I get from her.
> Q: The same sort of words, is she mimicking [his] words?
> A: *Exactly the same.*

Hearing her young daughter mouth the same abusive words her partner had used against her distressed Nolene but was something she worked hard to try to understand and respond to without retaliating with anger or cruelty.

Katrina had a different parental worry indicating that it was only after they had separated from her abusive partner that she realised the extent of her eldest son's abuse:

> Yeah, it wasn't until I left that I realised the depth of it, but most of it was directed towards my eldest son… He's [eldest son] from a previous relationship, yeah…I honestly think he [ex-partner] was threatened by my relationship with him because I'm so close with my son, we're best friends and I think he was threatened by him. Even though my son is so placid. I mean he was scared of him, he never even raised his voice or questioned anything that he ever said; I really think that he was just threatened by the closeness and he knew that my kids came first, he knew that I'd choose my kids over him any day.

> Q: And you did.
> A: And I did. And I'd do it again in a heartbeat, I should've done it earlier, yeah. And that's my only regret—is staying so long.

While still carrying guilt at not leaving her violent spouse sooner, Katrina nevertheless took pride in the fact that she had eventually done so. It was a very different experience for Jacqui, Stella, and Allison, all of whom found their 'recovery period' more agonising than pride-inducing or empowering.

Managing the Aftermath

Even with clarity and good support, domestic violence victims may find the road ahead very difficult (Murray 2008). Paradoxically, victims/survivors may report being flooded with anxiety once they have relocated to a safer place (also see Herman 2015). Flashbacks, panic attacks, nightmares, and/or compulsions may also surface post-separation and cause havoc with survivors' appetite, sleep, capacity to work, and overall mental health (Herman 2015). Nolene was one of several women we interviewed for the *Loving You* project who indicated being confronted with many intense emotions post-separation, understanding it to be a way for the body to process trauma:

So, when it starts calming down a bit [post-separation], that's when it hits you. [It's] when your life is getting into balance and you're getting back on track again with … of normality, that's when all that stored up stuff comes to the fore.

Q: Seems so cruel doesn't it?

A: Yes and no, in all honesty, because it's a good thing. Because you realise what areas affected you the most, what areas – what – you realise with a trauma what the actual trauma was.

Q: It clarifies?

A: [Nods] And so then you can address it, and you draw strength on that going okay, these are areas that I did not know where problematic, so if I can work on them.

Jacqui, in particular, detailed the regrets, fears, and experiences of injustice she felt through experiencing domestic violence and being expected to flee the family home and live in relative poverty:

I regret the fact that I sold our house and started to build another one with him. What I should have done was kicked him out and kept that other house, because at least I'd have something. Now I have nothing because he ripped me off. He lives in a lovely place down there [points], with his girlfriend, playing happy families with my two kids when they come down. And I'm stuck here, I can barely make food on the table, I can't get a job because the job which I was in hospitality. I was a Manager. I can't do [those hours] with kids around. So, basically I'm starting again… and not getting ahead…. Does that make sense?

Q: Yeah it does that, on …, while you've got some improvements, you've also inherited some other problems from the separation.

A: Yeah….And I understand why a lot of people go back to their partners, because they think that, what's worse, that part or the loneliness part, or the nobody wants me part? Then there's the poverty part you know, so I get it. It's a terrible when I say this, but I understand why people get in the car with their kids and drive off the end of the jetty. I mean personally I wouldn't do it, I hope I wouldn't do it … but I understand why they do do it—because they see that dark hole and think there's no way of getting out of it.

Talking about driving off the jetty with her children in the car may have been an off-the-cuff comment by Jacqui that she quickly disavowed ("I wouldn't do it"). Yet such catastrophic events do happen, and with greater frequency than people might realise (see Logan et al. 2013).

Both the fear and actual risk of becoming homeless after experiencing domestic violence is well established in Australia (Cameron 2015; Victorian Government 2016) and internationally (also see Baker et al. 2010). For instance, Baker et al. (2003) from Georgia in the US conducted a study with 110 women survivors of domestic violence, about their experiences of housing and homelessness. Of these women, 38% reported homelessness, with more experiencing related problems, such as going without meals to pay rent and/or being threatened with eviction (Baker et al. 2003).

Nolene reported that housing was a major problem that produced a cascade of other problems. She was unable to stay living at her parents' house after she fled her abusive partner. She was also unable to find an affordable private rental for herself, her son and their two cats. This unstable housing situation was used against her in family court:

> So, for 10 months after [she left ex-partner]– because I couldn't find a place, even though I'm in the domestic violence, I'm with [domestic violence support service] and they're looking around so hard, because I am homeless. My parents couldn't take me in because of the threats … They couldn't take me in.

> Q: And the family court had already said that you had to be within 20 kilometres of radius [of her ex-partner]?
> A: Exactly.

Above, Nolene noted her appreciation of her support worker trying 'so hard.' This is important to recognise, given large bodies of evidence, across fields and modes of health and welfare practice, show that it is the quality of the worker/helping/therapeutic alliance—more than any perspective or intervention framework—most likely to influence clients' perceptions of progress made with nominated problem/s, their level of satisfaction with service provided, and perceptions of recovery and healing (see Goodman et al. 2016). For Nolene, this relationship mattered even though the worker was unable to stop what was to come next. We knew that Nolene had breached the court requirement that she remain living within a 20-km radius of her ex-partner. So, we asked:

Q: So, what happened?
A: The courts ended up changing – changing the custody – so for 10 months I was without my child.

The consequences for breaching the court order were severe. Primary custody of their son now lay with Nolene's violent ex-partner.

Q: So, you had him weekends and he [ex-partner] had him [during the week]?
A: Mmhm.
Q: So, they [family court] did what they said they were going to do?
A: Yep. The [domestic violence support service] worked so hard. I managed to find a place in January, they found me this one. The courts wouldn't even change it.
Q: No? … So then was the argument, "Well your son's been living with your ex – so he's settled, so we don't want to upset him-
A: *Oh bullshit my son was settled! He had 3 times in the Women's and Children's-*
Q: What for? Injuries?
A: Because he had panic attacks, because of bruises. Because of the panic attacks, to such a violent extent that he shut himself down. He would wee himself, because he was so frightened. He would just physically lose control of his bowels. It was these 2 cats that brought him back from the brink of nothing. Because they weren't just, they would not let anyone go near him. They would not let anyone go near him, and he would just sit there, when he was in a state, he would end up, he would end up so bad when he came back from his dad, that I couldn't touch him, couldn't touch him.
Q: Because he'd recoil?
A: Mmhm – and the only thing that brought him out of it was [cat], would curl up around him. That was the only thing.

Nolene (above) shows how abuse can continue post-separation, how domestic violence can produce a cascade of negative effects, including those associated with the family law court. Her story also shows how powerful the empathic love of companion animals can be for humans, such as her traumatised young son.

Recovery and Companion Animals

Throughout this book we have noted how companion animals can help assuage human loneliness and strengthen feelings of belonging—how touching, stroking, grooming, playing with, talking to, and otherwise interacting with companion animals has well-established physical and emotional benefits for humans and in some instances for the animals as well (Friedman et al. 2010). *The Loving You* participants were keen to underline this point, with many attributing their survival of the violence to their animal companions. Consider, for example, Allison, who said that post-separation

> I wouldn't be halfway here with, as I am now if it wasn't for him [Freddy]. He is my healing process. He's therapy in a sense. because I have a hard time admitting that I have mental health issues. Because of what I've been through, sometimes you're not talking. Just being with him is enough. Some people don't understand that, [they say] "Go see a therapist, go do this, go do that." These last few months [I've been] talking about it all the time. I have a case file now that I've had people write letters for me so I don't have to keep repeating. Because it [recounting the violence] just brings it back to the forefront.

The close emotional bonds that exist between many humans and their companion animals can intensify during times of crisis, including when experiencing domestic violence (e.g., Ascione et al. 2007; Fitzgerald 2007). To quote Allison, "anxiety is crippling. You can't even breathe sometimes and you can't even explain why." This, along with (deliberate) isolation from other sources of emotional support enforced by abusers, means that threats to harm companion animals can be effective tactics for coercive control (Volant et al. 2008). Jacqui noticed her dog's reaction to domestic violence only after they had left their family home and described the love she felt for him as superior to the love shared among humans:

Yeah, so he [dog] was like my baby…Davey, a collie dog. He's the one that's went through everything with me, domestic violence. So, without Davey I wouldn't have realised the amount that dogs pick up. It took me a while after Davey passed away to get Charlie [dog]. I needed Charlie, because I just needed the licks on the face. Because kids yell and scream at you, and they hurt you. Whereas he's [dog] got unconditional love and he licks me all the time and when I'm down, so it's like, do you know what I mean-

Q: Gives you that love?
A: Yeah. Cosy's up on the bed with me. So, when my kids aren't with me, it's almost like I have a brother or a sister with me, it's just, yeah. It's like having a man without dealing with crap…

Stella also described how close she felt to her dog and how uncomplicated the loyalty of this relationship was, including during the times when the domestic violence escalated:

She [my former Mastiff dog] went everywhere with me. Absolutely everywhere. She was blind too…and everyone loved her. She was really, was so good. I took her just about everywhere I went and she was, I was in another domestic violence relationship. So yeah, she's seen it all.

Q: Was that person cruel to her?
A: No, he looked after her really good.
Q: So, he was only cruel to you?
A: Yep… I think he was cruel to the dog that came after… Because she hated him.

Stella's excerpt above illustrates that human violence expressed towards animals is not always a precursor to violence perpetrated against humans but can occur afterwards (or not at all) when human victims leave. Stella's perception of her ex-partner's capacity to harm the other dog that came after her departure was informed by her observations of the next dog's reaction to him, which she worded strongly as "she hated him."

However, connections with companion animals can also diminish during adversity, possibly a reflection of compassion fatigue. Linda reflected with remarkable honesty on how she was not always able to connect with companion animals, that it depended on what else was happening at home. In the excerpt below she describes her own experiences of entering motherhood as a teenager, wanting to give her children as much as she could, including the chance to love companion animals, but not necessarily having the time, energy, or emotional space to connect with them, especially as her husband's abuse escalated:

> So, my first child was born when I was 15, 16… No, no time for high school. No time for growing up.
>
> Q: Straight in to motherhood.
> A: Straight into motherhood and trying to work out what was going on sort of thing. So no, no real animals, no real connection you could say, never real connected with another animal in that sense like I had. My next animal you could say was like a little Jack Russell. Tried to connect but didn't have that connection because between the ex or my husband, the kids and trying to work out with the dog or cats or anything like that just wasn't fitting in.
> Q: Too much responsibility?
> A: Yeah, yeah big time but the kids had the animals. I knew how important it was for me growing up and what I got out of the relationship. Whenever the kids had asked I'd say yes because I knew how important an animal can be to – because the kids didn't – what I grew up with the kids sort of – that – the kids grew up with it as well, domestic violence, drugs, alcohol, that sort of stuff. So I knew how important having a companion whether it be a cat, dog, bird [or] whatever, [it] was really important.

Contexts—not just individual intentions—mediate the type and quality of connections humans and companion animals are able to share. As shown with Linda's stories, there are times in people's lives that can be more conducive to fully caring for, not just loosely caring about, the companion animals living with them. Linda's stories show how connected she was to her childhood dog Zac, but then with early motherhood, her connections to subsequent animals lessened. We know from our interview with her that once inside a women's prison, Linda stumbled into a greyhound rehabilitation programme and had her love of dogs reawakened (for information on the programme, see Debelle 2016).

Maintaining the Will to Live

Post-separation, Stella also reported feeling a crushing sense of loneliness and isolation and struggled not to internalise responsibility for her marital relationship breaking down (also see Holt 2016). The strength of connection she felt for her children helped but then there were the times when they stayed with their father. Stella reported that these times were the worst and how important her cats have been to her 'doing something stupid':

> I just think that it's easier to get through with, if you – when you've got kids. Because they go to the parents, the other parents on the weekend or something and then you're left alone. So they, I think they help get through the trauma and everything a lot quicker.... Yeah. I think, because I have been in really low places and having them [the cats] has stopped me doing shit, something stupid [such as self-harming].

Allison was also struggling with serious mental health issues she attributed to surviving domestic violence, making her post-separation experience a misery. Allison recounted the time she attempted suicide the year before and was subsequently detained. It was the night she received an eviction order to leave her rental property.

> That night, it was probably 2 nights before the Sheriff's office were due to come, even though I'd paid all my rent up, they still wanted me out. I couldn't understand it, until afterward when they told me it's because of the neighbour across the road kept calling the police and it was, they were friends with the landlord. But I took 8 Seroquel, a bottle of wine and probably about 30 Valium. I knew that would do the trick—if you do alcohol and drugs together. I do remember him [dog] howling and trying to lick my face and stuff. I was crying, thinking that I can't come back though. And then I woke up to some paramedics slapping my face...

Allison then described how she was admitted to hospital but discharged herself shortly after regaining consciousness. She did this because she was concerned about her dog, only to find the police arriving on her doorstep a few hours later to detain her:

And I'm off my head at this point. Those Seroquel [sleeping tablets] was brutal, absolutely brutal. I don't know how I did it, but I did. I got home with all intentions of just getting the rest of my shit and my dog and hopefully getting out of there. But I fell asleep. And I woke up to the police at the door with a piece of paper, a Section 32. I'm like "shit!" I didn't want to go.

Q: They detained you?
A: [Nodding]. They detained me. That was the worst thing ever because, it was probably my worst nightmare… I got restrained and a needle in the butt and hard night for me and next morning first thing I thought of was him. "I've got to go, got to go, got to get my dog."

Being reunited with her dog was so important to Allison because he soothed her and helped her maintain the will to live (also see Walsh and Mertin 1994):

Had I not had him [Freddy] for this past year and a half I probably would have, probably succeeded in killing myself I actually do.

Q: He's kept you alive?
A: *He still does.*
Q: Why do you reckon that is?
A: It's just pure love it's, it's to me that I'm at least loved, by something because he, he can, dogs sense things, he senses things. When I OD'd in November which was on purpose, your heart rate slows and dogs can sense that. And he was, he sat there and licked my face for hours and was howling and everything to try and get someone's attention-
Q: To get help?
A: *Yeah.…*

Jacqui expressed similar sentiments to Allison, but in relation to her cat:

He [cat] helped me keep me alive … He gave me the strength to hold on until I could figure out whether I could do it on my own or not … Yeah because he sat and listened to me – the poor thing. I'm not really sure if he had a choice because he has arthritis, but right at the end I would go outside and I would talk to him [there].

Nolene also underlined the life-affirming connections she felt with companion animals, and how important these relationships have been for her forging a new life away from her (violent) ex-partner:

> When you're feeling so unlovable, when your whole life has been ripped, and in those times when you're just so lonely … when I used to cry, when I used to, when it was just too much, and it took ages for me to cry, but sitting in the shower, and I just burst into tears, and he would just be sitting right there with me, or that 1 paw that they do, that 1 paw on you.... It is the best feeling in the world.

Yet, as discussed in Chap. 5, we must not forget that while animal companions are assisting humans to recover from violence, they are likely to need support for their own recovery, including those animals whose experience of violence also involved neglect (see Lockwood and Arkow 2016).

Conclusion

From our studies and from many others' work, we know that domestic violence is a potentially life-limiting and life-threatening experience for human and animal victims, and that chronic abuse can take a heavy toll on victims. We also know that for many, trying to make an escape and then trying to recover from the trauma of domestic violence can be difficult processes to navigate. For many victims/survivors, there is no simple escape, nor straightforward recovery to be enjoyed. Further distress and anxiety are likely, not just in relation to housing, finances, custody arrangements, and immediate safety concerns but also in relation to attempts to rebuild the self and relationships with others post-separation.

Our research participants (and others) emphasised that in spite of the rhetoric admonishing victims to 'just leave,' help can be elusive. Current service provisions for victims of domestic violence can involve pot-luck. Policy and operational matters that exist well beyond victims' control will dictate whether formal help is available in or near where victims live, whether it is available at the time when victims need it, and whether it includes non-human members of the family. The women participants in the *Loving You* project 'got lucky' where pet-friendly accommodation was concerned. Some had to first suffer the challenges of living day to day in a motel while they waited to become a client of the Northern Domestic Violence Service, who partnered with us in this study (see NDVS 2013). This help, and the emotional support of their workers who understood not just how domestic violence can hurt a human but also how it can hurt animals, was crucial for these women. We have also shown in this chapter just some of the roles that companion animals can play in helping humans in recovery. However, as we have stressed throughout this book, taking animal victims of domestic violence seriously necessitates that we must also consider the impact on them of their humans' mental health and sometimes chaotic lives. We take this point up further in the final chapter.

References

Anderson, M. A., Gillig, P. M., Sitaker, M., McCloskey, K., Malloy, K., & Grigsby, N. (2003). "Why doesn't she just leave?": A descriptive study of victim-reported impediments to her safety. *Journal of Family Violence, 18*(3), 151–155.

Ascione, F., Weber, C. V., Thompson, T. M., Heath, J., Maruyama, M., & Hayashi, K. (2007). Battered pets and domestic violence: Animal abuse reported by women experiencing intimate partner violence and by nonabused women. *Violence Against Women, 14*(4), 354–373.

Baker, C. K., Cook, S. L., & Norris, F. H. (2003). Domestic violence and housing problems: A contextual analysis of women's help-seeking, received informal support, and formal system response. *Violence Against Women, 9*(7), 754–783.

Baker, C. K., Billhardt, K. A., Warren, J., Rollins, C., & Glass, N. E. (2010). Domestic violence, housing instability, and homelessness: A review of housing policies and program practices for meeting the needs of survivors. *Aggression and Violent Behavior, 15*(6), 430–439.

Berns, N. S. (2017). *Framing the victim: Domestic violence, media, and social problems.* New York: Routledge.

Bowyer, L., Swanston, J., & Vetere, A. (2015). Eventually you just get used to it': An interpretative phenomenological analysis of 10–16 year-old girls' experiences of the transition into temporary accommodation after exposure to domestic violence perpetrated by men against their mothers. *Clinical Child Psychology and Psychiatry, 20*(2), 304–323.

Cameron, P. (2015). From safe refuge to safe at home: The evolving role of family violence outreach services. *Parity, 28*(1), 18.

Crisafi, D. N., & Jasinski, J. L. (2016). Within the bounds: The role of relocation on intimate partner violence help-seeking for immigrant and native women with histories of homelessness. *Violence Against Women, 22*(8), 986–1006.

Debelle, P. (2016, August 26). Heal girl, Greyhound Adoption Program helping inmates at Adelaide's Women's Prison. *news.com.au.* Retrieved August 5, 2018, from https://www.news.com.au/national/south-australia/heal-girl-greyhound-adoption-program-helping-inmates-at-adelaides-womens-prison/news-story/e069a1516ac1ca5f02da24be3cd31834

Evans, M. A., & Feder, G. S. (2016). Help-seeking amongst women survivors of domestic violence: A qualitative study of pathways towards formal and informal support. *Health Expectations, 19*(1), 62–73.

Fanslow, J. L., & Robinson, E. M. (2010). Help-seeking behaviors and reasons for help seeking reported by a representative sample of women victims of intimate partner violence in New Zealand. *Journal of Interpersonal Violence, 25*(5), 929–951.

Fitzgerald, A. J. (2007). "They gave me a reason to live": The protective effects of companion animals on the suicidality of abused women. *Humanity and Society, 31*(4), 355–378.

Fraser, H. (1999, July). Considering the needs of children who are exposed to domestic violence: A feminist perspective for practitioners. *Women Against Violence: An Australian Feminist Journal*, (6), 34.

Fraser, H. (2005). Women, love, and intimacy "gone wrong": Fire, wind, and ice. *Affilia, 20*(1), 10–20.

Fraser, H. (2008). *In the name of love, women's narratives of love and abuse.* Toronto: Women's Press.

Friedman, E., Son, H., & Tsai, C. C. (2010). The animal/human bond: Health and wellness. In A. Fine (Ed.), *Handbook on animal-assisted therapy: Theoretical foundations and guidelines for practice* (pp. 85–107). Oxford: Academic Press.

Fugate, M., Landis, L., Riordan, K., Naureckas, S., & Engel, B. (2005). Barriers to domestic violence help seeking: Implications for intervention. *Violence Against Women, 11*(3), 290–310.

García-Moreno, C., Jansen, H., Ellsberg, M., Heise, L., & Watts, C. (2005). *WHO multi-country study on women's health and domestic violence against women*. Geneva: World Health Organization.

Goodman, L. A., Fauci, J. E., Sullivan, C. M., DiGiovanni, C. D., & Wilson, J. M. (2016). Domestic violence survivors' empowerment and mental health: Exploring the role of the alliance with advocates. *American Journal of Orthopsychiatry, 86*(3), 286–296.

Harne, L., & Radford, J. (2008). *Tackling domestic violence: Theories, policies and practice*. Berkshire: Open University Press.

Herman, J. L. (2015). *Trauma and recovery: The aftermath of violence: From domestic abuse to political terror*. New York: Hachette.

Holt, S. (2016). Domestic violence and the paradox of post-separation mothering. *British Journal of Social Work, 47*(7), 2049–2067.

Johnson, M. P. (2010). *A typology of domestic violence: Intimate terrorism, violent resistance, and situational couple violence*. Lebanon: Northeastern University Press.

Lockwood, R., & Arkow, P. (2016). Animal abuse and interpersonal violence: The cruelty connection and its implications for veterinary pathology. *Veterinary Pathology, 53*(5), 910–918.

Logan, J. E., Walsh, S., Patel, N., & Hall, J. E. (2013). Homicide-followed-by-suicide incidents involving child victims. *American Journal of Health Behavior, 37*(4), 531–542.

Murray, S. (2002). *More than refuge: Changing responses to domestic violence*. Crawley: University of Western Australia Press.

Murray, S. (2008). "Why doesn't she just leave?": Belonging, disruption and domestic violence. *Women's Studies International Forum, 31*(1), 65–72.

National Link Coalition. (n.d.). *Domestic violence and animal cruelty*. Retrieved August 10, 2018, from http://nationallinkcoalition.org/resources/articles-research#DOMESTIC%20VIOLENCE

Northern Domestic Violence Service (NDVS). (2013). *Welcome to NDVS*. Retrieved August 10, 2018, from http://www.ndvs.asn.au/

O'Haire, M. E. (2012). Pets as a prescription for health: The benefits of companion animals for mental well-being. *Mental Notes, 6*(3), 5–7.

Owen, S., & Carrington, K. (2015). Domestic violence service provision and the architecture of rural life: An Australian case study. *Journal of Rural Studies, 39*, 229–238.

Peckover, S. (2003). 'I could have just done with a little more help': An analysis of women's help-seeking from health visitors in the context of domestic violence. *Health & Social Care in the Community, 11*(3), 275–282.

Rhodes, N. R., & McKenzie, E. B. (1998). Why do battered women stay? Three decades of research. *Aggression and Violent Behavior, 3*(4), 391–406.

Richardson, F. (2016). The Victorian royal commission into family violence. *Parity, 29*(4), 6–7.

Roomani, F. Z., Tayyab, F., Kamal, N., & Siddique, K. (2016). Role of women in perpetuating violence against women: Case studies of domestic violence victims. *Pakistan Journal of Social Sciences (PJSS), 36*(2), 1185–1195.

Rose, D., Trevillion, K., Woodall, A., Morgan, C., Feder, G., & Howard, L. (2011). Barriers and facilitators of disclosures of domestic violence by mental health service users: Qualitative study. *The British Journal of Psychiatry, 198*(3), 189–194.

Strauchler, O., McCloskey, K., Malloy, K., Sitaker, M., Grigsby, N., & Gillig, P. (2004). Humiliation, manipulation, and control: Evidence of centrality in domestic violence against an adult partner. *Journal of Family Violence, 19*(6), 339–346.

The Links Group (UK). (n.d.). *Welcome to the links group.* Retrieved October 8, 2018, from http://www.thelinksgroup.org.uk/

Theobald, J., Murray, S., & Smart, J. (2017). *From the margins to the mainstream: The domestic violence services movement in Victoria, Australia, 1974–2016.* Melbourne: Melbourne University Press.

Tiplady, C., Walsh, D., & Phillips, C. (2015). The ongoing impact of domestic violence on animal welfare. *Animal Studies Journal, 4*(2), 116–139. Retrieved August 13, 2018, from http://ro.uow.edu.au/asj/vol4/iss2/6

Vandello, J. A., & Cohen, D. (2003). Male honor and female fidelity: Implicit cultural scripts that perpetuate domestic violence. *Journal of Personality and Social Psychology, 84*(5), 997–1010.

Victorian Government. (2016). *Royal commission into family violence, summary and recommendations,* Retrieved August 18, 2018, from http://www.rcfv.com.au/MediaLibraries/RCFamilyViolence/Reports/Final/RCFV-Summary.pdf

Victorian Government, Rent Fair Victoria: Pets are Welcome. Retrieved September 24, 2018, from https://www.vic.gov.au/rentfair/pets-are-welcome.html

Volant, A. M., Johnson, J. A., Gullone, E., & Coleman, G. J. (2008). The relationship between domestic violence and animal abuse: An Australian study. *Journal of Interpersonal Violence, 23*(9), 1277–1295.

Walsh, P. G., & Mertin, P. G. (1994). The training of pets as therapy dogs in a women's prison: A pilot study. *Anthrozoös, 7*(2), 124–128.

Wuerch, M. A., Giesbrecht, C. J., Price, J. A., Knutson, T., & Wach, F. (2017). Examining the relationship between intimate partner violence and concern for animal care and safekeeping. *Journal of Interpersonal Violence*, online first, https://doi.org/10.1177/0886260517700618

Yamawaki, N., Ochoa-Shipp, M., Pulsipher, C., Harlos, A., & Swindler, S. (2012). Perceptions of domestic violence: The effects of domestic violence myths, victim's relationship with her abuser, and the decision to return to her abuser. *Journal of Interpersonal Violence, 27*(16), 3195–3212.

Fig. 7.1 Woman watching cat on floor

7

The Work of Significant Other/s: Companion Animal Relationships in the Future

Introduction

Earlier in this book we underlined the significance of family/domestic violence, including the many costs to both individuals and society. We also noted the ongoing problem of it being under-reported (Bunting et al. 2010). Our message throughout this book is that domestic violence has been and still is a serious, complex public problem requiring massive ongoing, collective response efforts. We say this as feminists who became adults during the second wave of feminism, and who are proud to have been part of the British (Nik) and Australian (Heather) women's movements that helped to put domestic violence on the public map of social problems (see Nixon and Humphreys 2010). In the discussion below, we reflect on some of the changes we have observed. While these are welcome changes, the message from this reflection is that it is important to extend—and keep extending—feminist understandings of domestic violence: in this case, to recognise animals as victims of domestic violence.

© The Author(s) 2019
N. Taylor, H. Fraser, *Companion Animals and Domestic Violence*, Palgrave Studies in Animals and Social Problems, https://doi.org/10.1007/978-3-030-04125-0_7

Half a Century of Campaigns, Research, and Service Provision

In Anglo-American dominated countries such as Australia, we have now had a half-century of advancements in knowledge, policy making, and service provision that have helped improve our collective understanding of and responses to domestic violence. Compared to when we first undertook women's studies courses in the 1980s (Heather) and 1990s (Nik), huge bodies of work about domestic violence have been produced, including feminist works that have provided many conceptual, theoretical, practical, and political insights.

Since I (Heather) started working in a women's refuge 35 years ago, much more is understood and on offer. Back in the mid-1980s, while working in the Para Districts' Women's Shelter (PDWS) (Elizabeth, South Australia—the precursor to NDVS), I remember us coming to grips with the extent and severity of the problem. The Shelter was relatively new, funding meagre, and community understanding of the need for such service offerings was generally low. It was staffed by women and run as a collective with funding almost exclusively for women. Children were not individually counted as clients until the early 2000s, reflective of a broader trend in social work at that time to see child abuse and domestic violence as separate issues (McKay 1994).

PDWS was located in an outer suburb in an ordinary street, not obvious to most apart from the taxi drivers, police, and neighbours who learned of its purpose. In spite of many efforts to go unnoticed, violent spouses regularly appeared outside the shelter threatening further violence if their spouse did not come outside. In turn, this intensified pressures from neighbours, some of whom expressed their displeasure to local politicians at having to live near the refuge. Some police in our local area were allies and provided support during these times, while others scoffed at our requests, dismissing them as 'private domestic incidents.' There were no special units, policies, or police training in domestic violence. Knowledge about domestic violence was rudimentary and difficult to disseminate. While we had printed newsletters, badges, and T-shirts and organised sit-ins and street protests to get attention and spread our messages, there were no smartphones or apps with information to quickly and secretly access.

As white women working in the PDWS, we were yet to learn about white privilege and theories about disablism were under-developed. So, we provided services to mostly white, working-class women and their children, who were crammed into single bedrooms in two adjoining home units. Women who drank alcohol or used other substances were prohibited from residing in the shelter, and for residents who got intoxicated, eviction was likely. What we knew about the connections between domestic violence, racism, and substance abuse, mental health problems and poverty came from experience not university education, professional development, research or journal articles. Questions about women's complicity in the violence—their/our predisposition to passivity, hysteria, and masochism—played out in many heated discussions, including debates about the implications of supporting the legal defence of *battered wives' syndrome* (see Swanson 1984) and *learned helplessness* (see Alexander 1993).

From the 1970s to the late 1980s, it was common to portray as radical women who left their husbands and those of us who supported them to do so. Across the client/worker divide, the horror of what we collectively saw happening to women within the supposed safety of their own homes did radicalise many of us, making some of us strident and polemical about patriarchy (also see Nixon and Humphreys 2010). The more we looked around, the more we could see male dominance in all quarters of our lives—in our homes, workplaces, churches, health, welfare, legal and education institutions, and public spaces. It was hard not to be enraged, especially since the general public was still largely blind to the problem.

Working for the PDWS, on the frontline of domestic violence in an impoverished outer suburb involved dramatic, unforgettable experiences. Thirty years later, I (Heather) can still recall visiting women in hospital whose faces were unrecognisable from the trauma 'their men' had inflicted on them. I can also remember the first time I helped a young woman flee her father's violence, accompanied by several young children whom he had fathered. Relatively little was known by the public about 'incest' and it was thought to be a rare occurrence (see Frances and Frances 1976). In these intensely emotive circumstances, our rage often meant vilifying male perpetrators of violence, a practice that Corvo and Johnson (2003) objected to, noting that it obstructs our capacity to work more holistically with family members, including those who are violent.

Since the 1980s we have personally witnessed the growth in research examining different forms of domestic violence, including but not limited to children's exposure to domestic violence, elder abuse, sibling abuse, abuse by extended kin, rape in marriage and other forms of intimate partner violence (IPV). Since the 1990s our collective, interdisciplinary, inter-professional appreciation of how domestic violence affects different groups and subgroups of humans has produced important breakthroughs in understanding the socio-cultural, not just relational and intrapersonal aspects of domestic violence. Slowly, there has been an understanding that domestic violence is not just about interpersonal relations or individual victims' psychology, and that the economic and cultural empowerment of victims, through education, training, paid employment, and liveable incomes can be protective factors against domestic violation, especially chronic forms of it (see Jewkes 2002; Michau et al. 2015). Studies about domestic violence have proliferated, including those focusing on specific populations, such as children, and those considering the future ramifications of chronic exposure (see Holt et al. 2008; McKay 1994; Swanston et al. 2014). The past five decades of international work done in relation to violence against women have produced more nuanced feminist understandings, especially about how different groups of women victims/survivors are affected. This includes more attention to domestic violence across the lifespans, such as it is experienced by young women (see Stöckl et al. 2014) and older women (see Crockett et al. 2015), and across categories of difference, such as women with disabilities (see Breiding and Armour 2015) and women of diverse genders and sexuality (see Perryman and Appleton 2016; Renzetti and Miley 2014).

Today more is known about the material and cultural obstacles to safety for people who are gender and/or sexuality diverse. For people of diverse genders and sexualities there is also the problem of being excluded from dominant discourses about who is likely to commit domestic violence, and who is likely to suffer it (Renzetti and Miley 2014; Taylor et al. 2017). This can affect not just the willingness of non-heterosexual populations to present for help from social welfare agencies dedicated to addressing domestic violence, but also the policy and service offerings made available to them (Renzetti and Miley 2014; Taylor et al. 2017). Additional problems are likely, including structural problems associated with homophobia and bullying in schools and workplace; restricted employment opportunities and work rights; and, until recently, legal discrimination associated with marriage, deaths, and wills (see Riggs et al. 2018).

Racial, ethnic, and/or migrant status and susceptibility to domestic violence have been cross-tabulated to show the common reactions and implications (see Krug et al. 2002). Concerted efforts have been made to better understand how Indigenous communities are affected by family violence (Cheers et al. 2006), for example, including those who are located in rural and remote locations, and those who seek restorative justice (Nancarrow 2006) and community-building rather than criminalised individual responses (Cheers et al. 2006).

Several biomedical and other non-feminist accounts of domestic violence have also emerged, including those that posit how men and women can be equally abusive (for a critique, see Kelly and Westmarland 2016; Taft et al. 2001). From the mountain of evidence accrued across the world, along with diverse theoretical constructions, we can all agree that prevention, early detection, and intervention can help reduce their ongoing likelihood and negative effects (see Breiding and Armour 2015).

At least officially, domestic violence has moved from being a woman's (personal) issue to a widespread, multi-faceted (public) priority for the World Health Organization and national health agendas (Taft et al. 2001). An expression of this is studying domestic violence in relation to questions about the differential burden of disease by specified populations (see Krug et al. 2002). This includes groups who comprise much smaller statistical populations of victims, such as heterosexual men abused by female intimates, who may still have their experiences denied or trivialised, which can leave them alone, ashamed, and unsupported (Perryman and Appleton 2016). These nuanced understandings and investigations are to be welcomed while still acknowledging that much more needs to be done.

The purpose of making these comments is not to stray from our focus on gender, species, and to a lesser extent class—specifically working-class women and companion animals' experiences of surviving domestic violence together. Rather, it has been to reflect on the extensive developments in domestic violence knowledge building, social policy making, and service provision. Our point is that while insights have been plentiful, further work is required, particularly in terms of including other species in our understanding and responses. Nixon and Humphreys (2010) call for an updating of the feminist frame for a more intersectional understanding of domestic violence, one that pays more attention to the material, not just psychological, realities of impoverished and/or ethnically/racialised minority women. We accept this call but are arguing that there is a need to go still further: to include animals in the purview of domestic violence victimisation.

This is an argument we have made throughout this book by putting forward alternative—feminist intersectional—understandings of domestic violence, focusing on two marginalised groups: companion animals and women. Our arguments have been drawn broadly from feminism, post-humanism, social work, and sociology, and are located within critical feminist and animal studies. For explanatory purposes we use three overlapping and intersecting focal points to summarise our arguments: (1) theories, (2) methods, and (3) practices.

Theories: Animals and Feminist Intersectionality

Concepts from feminist intersectionality helped us to theoretically frame and analyse the projects from which we have drawn data. This has included speciesism as an axis of structural oppression (for animals) and unearned privilege (for humans). As Hovorka (2015, 5) explains, "Both sexism and speciesism produce a 'saming' and 'othering' of women and animals, denying them rationality, agency and history (relative to men and humans) and enabling a moral detachment that creates and perpetuates oppressive practices and institutions." Feminism has eschewed this detachment, instead developing the idea of scholar-activism. For decades feminists have pointed out that no work—especially social science work—is value-free or neutral and that siding with the underdog through trying to illuminate the realities of others' lives can be good scholarship (see Chap. 3).

Focusing on companion animals throughout this book is one of the many ways needed to highlight the mechanisms of oppression and power that underpin domestic violence. While we accept there have been limitations (see Chap. 3), we have tried to make visible the women and the animals that were a part of our research through the women's stories about themselves and their companion animals. This visibility is important as we advocate for an increasing awareness of the impact of domestic violence on animals not just humans. Linked to this is our attempt to include the animals as individuals, where possible, using their names to distinguish their individuality and including their stories too, as best we can (also see Hamilton and Taylor 2017). Visual images that focus on the animals have also been used on the front page of each chapter and the inclusion of descriptive reminders of non-human-like behaviours have been used to signal species differences, such as dogs sniffing and licking us, laying or standing across our laps, or cats perching on headrests, while we sat conducting the interviews.

We paid attention to the interactions we had with the animal participants, because from feminist scholarship we have

> learned to be affected long ago by viewing research subjects as active participants in knowledge production, embracing methods decreasing distance between the researcher and the subject, and seeking empathetic understanding of individual and collective standpoints. (Hovorka 2015, 10)

While our engagement with intersectionality has been pivotal to the book, it has, by necessity, been partial. It is more accurate to say that we used ideas from feminist intersectionality to theorise aspects of participants' reported experiences rather than claiming to have produced complete intersectional accounts. We concentrated on species, gender, and class mostly because the *Loving You* participants we met were working-class, cisgender, heterosexual women or companion animals. Future accounts using more comprehensive intersectional analyses might also consider the intersections of race/ethnicity, sexualities and genders, age, ability, religion, species differences, and geographical location.

Interspecies Love, Care, and Work

In addition to making visible intersections between gender, species, and class, we have conceptualised love and abuse as intersecting rather than opposing phenomena (see Chaps. 2 and 4). This offers us the chance to understand how love and abuse can coexist for humans and companion animals. This includes how feelings of love, loyalty, and fidelity can confuse and trap victims of domestic violence (also see Fraser 2008). We discussed the notions of interspecies empathic love and connections—relationships characterised by kindness, emotional attunement, respectful caregiving, and a willingness to suspend one's own interests for others. These micro practices of care and affection are evident in how we touch, talk to, consider, and engage companion animals and the other humans in their lives. They can show through our actions the recognition of companion animals as significant others.

Caring for others involves feelings and actions that "provide responsively for an individual's personal needs or well-being, in a face-to-face relationship" (Cancian and Oliker 2000, 2). Care work is an integral part of our societies, providing crucial infrastructure to all needing assistance and to family members who are otherwise obliged to provide that care (conventionally women). Yet care work, and the emotional labour it necessitates, has a long history of being devalued in Western societies largely because it has been perceived as 'women's work' that does not contribute to the economy the kind of value produced by other forms of work (Herd and Meyer 2002). This is the (so-called) 'devaluation view' (England et al. 2002): that care work is doubly devalued because it is not paid and because it is primarily done by women.

Critically analysing the intersections between love, work, and care calls for us to see beyond the false distinctions so often made between paid/unpaid work and volunteers/workers. It requires us to deconstruct the ideas that care work should be done for love, not money, or that caregiving is not 'real' work—that if it were, it would be paid for. It calls for us to challenge the misguided belief that anyone can do care work, that it is unskilled, low-status work. It prompts us to consider how some forms of work are ignored, trivialised, and undervalued, especially when performed by subordinated and devalued workers, such as 'housewives' and 'pets' (roles that can converge, such as young women's enactment of playboy bunnies). Research into the effects of care work on humans (mostly women) shows care workers often have poorer physical and mental health than their peers (Herd and Meyer 2002). One of the many reasons for this relates to the unpaid nature of informal caregiving and the underpayment of informal care work, both of which can lead to impoverished living conditions for carers. For many, it will also mean exclusion from the (limited) protections afforded by official laws and policies for paid workers (Coulter 2016a).

Exploring the conceptual and theoretical interconnections between love, care, and work is also instructive when conducted across the human/animal divide. Emotional receptivity, playful affection, and abiding loyalty are common—expected—features of animal companionship. In mainstream accounts of caregiving, the work performed by animal companions rarely rates a mention, or if it is mentioned may be represented as cute and toy-like (see Nicholas and Gullone 2001). By and large, animals' work is ignored, whether this is interpersonal work of the kind that we are discussing here, or the contribution their labour—and their bodies—make to the economy (Hamilton and Taylor 2013). While so many studies have shown the costs of domestic violence, including costs incurred to victims during recovery, but also wider costs to national economies, few recognise, count, or appreciate the work of animal companions. This is more than an oversight. Time and again we heard how companion animals helped humans recover from abuse. We heard how animals deliberately sought out children to soothe and care for them. For instance, *Loving You* participant Jacqui explained how her previous dog, who experienced violence along with her and her son, was the main source of support for her and how her son relies on their current dog for support—that he would "hug him like a teddy bear and not let him go, and just lay on him." Similarly, Katrina explained how Maddie, their dog, sleeps with the kids every night. Then, during the night, she'll go and do a round of the house and check on everybody. She's a real Mother to everybody. It just gives them a sense of peace. I couldn't imagine what it would be like without her, I think we'd struggle a lot without having just her to make us feel secure.

Often, animals are allies to women in post-abuse recovery because of their unqualified support, lack of judgement, unqualified love, and constant presence. Nolene from the *Loving You* project explained how one of her cats, Sam, was also always there for her:

When you're feeling so unlovable, when your whole life has been ripped, and in those times when you're just so lonely. You've seen him come up and do the circles, when I used to cry, when I used to, when it was just too much, and it took ages for me to cry, but sitting in the shower, and I just burst into tears, and he would just be sitting right there with me, or that 1 paw that they do, that 1 paw on you.

In Chap. 6 Allison explained how her dog Freddy not only keeps her alive through giving her emotional support but how he called attention to her when she deliberately overdosed.

Across all our companion animal studies (focus groups, interviews, online posts, and questionnaires) we were told how animals were appreciated for being 'on call' for their humans, how they help with depression by simply 'being there' and loving unconditionally and without judgement. However, as we have flagged throughout the book, we need to consider this from the animals' standpoint. Doing so means that we need to acknowledge that this might, in some circumstances, be a burden on animals who are themselves trying to recover from abuse. We encourage further research into these issues.

To be clear, our argument here is not that these animals need (necessarily) to be removed from their humans. Instead, it is that we need to ask theoretical questions about relationship fairness and the ethics of animal companionship. While we recognise the benefits for both species in maintaining their relationships post-abuse, it has become clear to us that animals are expected to do large amounts of emotional *labour* for their humans in post-abuse recovery. This was not something we were looking for and was not part of our original interview schedule. Instead, it became apparent through the women's stories about how the animals were part of their recovery. They used words such as 'healing process' and 'therapy.' As the project went on, we started to have some concerns about the amount of work that the animals were expected to do. While friendship between some humans and their animal companions is positive for both it is worth noting that an asymmetry exists where the animal is often or always 'on call' for humans, especially humans with high needs. It is worth asking what kind of a detrimental impact this might have on them.

The animals in our research are clearly involved in emotional and care work of/for their humans yet it goes largely unrecognised. As a result, there are very few safeguards for the animals in these situations (or, indeed, in formal 'therapeutic' arrangements) (Coulter 2016a). One particularly thorny issue among all this is that we 'own' animals so they have little protection under the law, and indeed Coulter (forthcoming) objects to the term 'partners' when considering animal labour for humans, as it is a term that obfuscates power asymmetries (the fact we 'own' animals). Despite this, she notes from her research that,

> regardless of what people call them, animals *are* friends, family members, allies, supporters, guardians, caregivers, mentors, enemies, survivors, agitators, and countless other identities, including workers ... I do not propose replacing the other, multiple identities—and subjectivities—animals possess with the singular category of worker ... I suggest identifying animals' work and their contributions as *another* dimension of their lives as individuals, species, and community members, as a way of thinking more widely and carefully about animals, about people, and about our connections. (Coulter 2016a, 146)

While there are similarities across animal and human care work, particularly regarding why they are ignored and/or devalued, there are also clear differences. Like us, Coulter is advocating for other animals and for their work to be taken seriously. This then provides a platform to consider their needs in and beyond that work. Coulter also adopts the idea of interspecies solidarity, noting that it can be put into practice in different ways; it is not a monolithic blueprint to be singularly imposed on all working lives or political projects. Rather, it is an invitation to broaden how labor as both a daily process and a political relationship are understood and approached. Accordingly, interspecies solidarity is both a path and the outline of a destination that encourages new ways of thinking and acting, individually and collectively, that are informed by empathy, support, dignity, and respect. (Coulter 2016a, 153; see also Coulter 2016b, c)

Part of extending the empathy, dignity, and respect that lead to interspecies solidarity involves seeing other species in the first place, or in the case of research *making* them visible.

Methods: Including Real 'Animals'

Methodologically we noted that much of the work that sits under the umbrella of 'animal studies' ignores real, fleshy, smelly, fun, dangerous, beautiful, live animals. Including the animals in our *Loving You, Loving Me* project and this book is our way of trying to recognise companion animals as embodied, agentic, sentient beings. Doing the home-based interviews allowed us to meet them, talk with them, stroke, and play with them. This involved visceral experiences of touch, smell, sound, and sight. Their periodic interruptions to the interviews—often playful and funny, as with the 15-year-old cat who constantly walked over our knees until her human pointed out that we were in her seat and she was demanding that we leave—drew our attention back to them and their individuality. Even so, we accept that there are several limitations to these interactions and do not wish to imply that our attempts to represent companion animals are unproblematic.

The exclusion of real animals from research in animal studies (and elsewhere) can be explained by our intellectual heritage that effectively writes animals out of the picture. In Western intellectual thought animals are assumed to be alingual, acultural, and creatures of instinct—dismissed as being of little importance to the constitution of human philosophy and epistemology. This pervasive anthropocentrism manifests itself in numerous ways; a relevant example that we have used throughout this book is in the consideration of animals as a 'red flag' to warn of potential human-human abuse, and to stop there. We have remained alert to this throughout the *Loving You* research process. As feminist scholars have reminded us time and again, and as we discussed in detail in Chap. 3, we owe an ethical debt to all our participants, both human and animal. Part of this means seeing and presenting their lives in context rather than as data sources we can mine. It also necessitates that we contemplate their experiences within the many constraints they experience. When focused on humans, this involves respectfully and carefully re-presenting speech, ideas, and stories that we gather as part of our data, as well as interrogating the researcher-participant relationship for power imbalances (Skeggs 1999). When focused on animals, it can start by looking for methods to make them visible.

For those of us interested in questioning implicit hierarchies between humans and other species however, this ethical concern is hard to realise in our research because animals don't tell stories, at least not as humans understand them. Animals can't be involved directly in traditional data collection methods, such as surveying or interviewing. Usually this means collecting data about them, such as human attitudes towards them. While understanding human attitudes towards animals is important, because it underpins our (often abhorrent) treatment of them, solely focusing on the human in the human-animal dyad writes animals out of research. The unintended effects are to silence, marginalise, and exclude them. We must therefore look for other methods, especially methods that show animals not just in relation to humans but in relation to each other. The traditional silencing and exclusion of other animals in our scholarly work is indicative of larger issues like species hierarchy, epistemic authority, and the power to create worldviews. Unwittingly or otherwise, we do this through our methods and our research that reinscribe human superiority. In relation to domestic violence, this is important because it is precisely this marginalising, excluding, and silencing that allows for them to be constructed as inferior to humans in the first place. The assumed superiority of humans and inferiority of animals creates a fertile ground for abuse.

Including real, fleshy, live animals in our research where possible allows us to counteract the view of animals as secondary to human interests. It allows us to represent their multiple agencies, interests, and rights which destabilises assumptions about power relations. It brings to the fore their lives, and their deaths, the disdain with which they are often treated or alternatively the love and affection we bestow on some companion animals. It reminds us that when we research and write about 'the animal condition' we are writing about the Freddy's, the Abbey's, and the Charlie's. It reminds us that these particular animals are *individuals* with personalities and idiosyncrasies all of their own.

We have tried—through the limited tools available to us—to give our research participants (human and animal) voice but without considering them as voiceless. This is because the notion of 'voicelessness' is highly problematic, particularly for other species. It is a fine line to walk between care and advocacy and casting animals as passive, voiceless victims—victims that we speak for. Yet avoiding this is important. As Spivak (1988) points out when we claim to 'speak for' 'voiceless' others, we commit a form of 'epistemic violence.' For her, this was where white man was constructed as saving victimised and voiceless brown women from brown men and was an operation of colonial oppression. Applying this to animals occurs when human-ness is discursively constituted as superior by those aiming to position themselves as voices for the voiceless. Sunaura Taylor (2017) links this to ableism, "But animals are too often presented simply as voiceless beings who suffer. Exploring their lives through a critical disability analysis can help us to ask who these animals are beyond their suffering". Other feminist scholars have also pointed out that speaking for animals who we cast as voiceless continues the kinds of behaviours we are trying to stop when calling attention to their abuse in the first place. Scholtmeijer (1996, 235) argues,

> 'humankind's root cultural relationship with animals is that of aggressor to victim. In narrative, as in life, it is difficult to escape the paradigm of victimization when it comes to animals. In narrative, animal victims make for dramatic action; often writers coopt animal tragedies to enhance the impression of pain in the world or simply to round out a plot. Indulgence in the narrative efficacy of killing an animal reinforces the conception of animals as congenital victims who call for the abuse they receive. Too often, the logic of the narrative affirms that the victimization of animals is only natural.

In discussing the role of fiction in bringing animals' and women's lives to the fore, she further argues that "establishing the legitimacy of outcast experiences is precisely the political cultural work that needs to be carried out in real life for the sake of all beings disenfranchised by sanctioned value systems" (1996, 233). This is why we chose to focus on women's stories that included narrations of their animals' lives and experiences.

Practices: Companion Animals As Significant Others

Understanding their lives and experiences in such ways is one way to advocate for animal victims of domestic violence to be seen. In turn this means they can start to be counted as important and supported. To achieve this, our policy and practice intervention methods need to expand. In terms of intervention methods, social policy, research, community work, group work, and casework are all needed to advance the recognition of (other) animals in domestic violence. Since measurement is so closely tied to justifications for funding, we need to count the number of animals affected by domestic violence as well as demonstrating how they are affected. To do this we may need to learn more about how various species display grief, anxiety (especially separation anxiety), and depression. With this information we can consider post-separation experiences of safety and protection—and the breaks or absences to these—which show just how risky it can be to try to flee violence, for both human and animal victims. While we are advocating, that this is done for animals who are victims of domestic violence, it need not stop there. It could, for instance, be extended to consider the impact on companion animals who are bred in 'puppy mills' (McMillan 2017), or on 'farm' animals lucky enough to be relocated to sanctuaries (Briefer and McElligott 2013).

We must continue to reflect on the common but also different ways in which violent family dynamics can play out 'in real life,' how they can affect real bodies—human and animal—and how we might intervene and respond to such dynamics. Often neglected but very important are housing and other material provisions that recognise that the concept of being a significant other can occur across species and should not be reserved only for humans.

To do this, several intervention methods are required. For instance, we can press for the creation of social policies and enactment of laws that reflect the lived experiences of the vast numbers of people who reside with companion animals and in rental housing. We can follow the lead of those in Victoria, Australia, making the case to constitute all rental housing as pet-friendly, where there would be an opt-out system for landlords who do not wish this to be so rather than an opt-in system that can mean less than 5% of available houses for rent permit companion animals (Victorian Government, Rent Fair Victoria).

We can do this in cross-sector partnerships, with domestic violence, child protection, and animal welfare sectors working in collaboration in cross-screening, reporting, supporting, and planning initiatives that recognise the interconnections in-and-between domestic violence, child abuse, elder abuse, and animal abuse. The *National Link Coalition* in the US has been showing us how to do this for more than 35 years, but in many other places these coordination efforts are not nearly as well developed. Central to these collaborations is the refusal to ignore the abuse and neglect of animals, or trivialise them, or see them as isolated incidents (National Link Coalition). Talking about the domestic violation of companion animals allows them to be noticed, counted, and responded to. Such talk can also open the door to other discussions of human-human violence, as (adult, human) victims may be more prepared to discuss the abuse of their animal companions than abuse directed towards themselves or their children, and neighbours may be more willing to report suspected animal abuse than violence against humans (National Link Coalition; Signal and Taylor 2008).

In Australia, consideration of the potential of the recognition of human-animal abuse for cross-reporting has yet to be developed. Yet, systems for cross-reporting abuse have many potential benefits:

1. Collecting additional data better equips researchers to quantify human/animal abuse (Long et al. 2007).
2. Including questions about animal cruelty in human welfare agency assessments provides useful information about family violence not forthcoming through existing channels.

3. A cross-reporting system allows for investigation in cases where individuals are banned from keeping animals. Currently no questions are asked about the risk of that person abusing their own children or other vulnerable individuals despite increased risk for human-directed abuse (Petersen and Farrington 2007).
4. Higher quality training and education efforts for professionals and sub-professionals, who through a common language created from interagency reporting, will be better placed to conduct assessments of perpetrator risk (Humphreys 2007) and other prevention or earlier intervention activities.
5. Incorporating animal well-being considerations (including pet fostering services) enables women and children to leave violent relationships (Ascione et al. 2007).
6. Including observations of, and/or questions about, animals in the home recognises the changing legal status of pets (as more than human property) and can improve interagency collaboration, strengthen the identification of families at high risk of violence, and guide referrals to appropriate services (Zilney and Zilney 2005).

In Australia cross-reporting human-animal abuse might start across three sectors (or domains): (1) human services (e.g., child protection and domestic violence policy makers and frontline practitioners); (2) animal welfare (e.g., policy makers and frontline workers from the Royal Society for the Prevention of Cruelty to Animals (RSPCA) and veterinary profession); and (3) law enforcement (e.g., criminal lawyers, police, correctional and probation officers). Beyond reporting suspected animal abuse, including their experiences of domestic violence, we need to ask questions about how we can assist the animals affected.

As this book nears its end we would like to emphasise that animal companionship can generate in humans an "immeasurable good" (Friedman et al. 2010). In earlier chapters we talked about the improved health and happiness humans often gain from keeping close company with animals (also see Morrison 2007; Pachana et al. 2005). Walsh (2009, 463) reminds us that this is not new:

In ancient times and in cultures worldwide, animals have been respected as essential partners in human survival, health, and healing. Many spiritual traditions have honored the relationships of people to animal forms of life, as part of the interconnectedness of the natural world and a link to the spirit world.

What is new is the number of scientific studies showing the significant contribution companion animals make to human health. For instance, companion animals are well-known social catalysts (Amiot et al. 2016), prompting interaction with other humans, and assuaging human loneliness (Banks and Banks 2002). Physiologically, they can improve humans' cardiovascular health and reduce stress (Allen et al. 2002; Nicholas and Gullone 2001). People who keep company with dogs, for instance, are usually more active, more socially connected to other humans, not just animals, and more inclined to participate in community activities (Headey 1999). People who live with cats often report doing so because of the affection and unconditional love they feel from their cats (Zasloff and Kidd 1994), in spite of the stereotypes of cats as aloof. Similar benefits are reported across other species lines, such as those accrued when humans connect with birds such as ducks and chickens (Every et al. 2017); rodents such as rats, mice, and Guinea pigs; and reptiles such as snakes and lizards (see Morrison 2007). To quote Allen et al. (2002, 735), "pets can buffer reactivity to acute stress as well as diminish perceptions of stress." Older human populations, in particular, are tuning in to the variety of benefits from caring for other animals in their places of residence. So popular are hens in a selection of Australian aged care facilities, for example, that the elderly residents refer to themselves not as pensioners but 'hensioners,' spending much of their day tending to and nursing individual hens (SBS 2016). These interspecies programmes have repeatedly shown that having the chance to care for another being, to have a relationship across species lines, and such a close one, is a major part of the appeal, especially for people spending extended periods at home (Banks and Banks 2002).

The paradox with companion animals is that while they are often praised in such studies and lauded in popular culture and social media as playmates, best friends, family members, and healers (see Flynn 2000;

Walsh 2009), they have largely escaped the attention of human service providers and social policy makers (Fook 2014; Risley-Curtiss 2010; Ryan 2011). This includes the field of domestic violence. This is a problem because it denies the lived experiences of so many, including some of the very disadvantaged victims of domestic violence we met (human and animal) trying to rebuild their lives after escaping violent households.

There are other anomalies and contradictions associated with eclipsing or invisibilising animals in domestic violence. For instance, in social work education and other social service training, there has been a long history constituting the 'social' in exclusively human terms (Risley-Curtiss 2010; Ryan 2011). This has occurred in spite of so many social workers, domestic violence support workers, and community workers personally identifying as 'animal lovers' (see Fook 2014). To conflate the social with human (and in so doing, exclude animals) ignores not just the needs and interests of animal victims but also those of the humans with whom they are significantly connected (Fook 2014; Morley and Fook 2005; Ryan 2011). The testimonies in this book from domestic violence victims are one important expression of this.

Not enabling social and support workers to collectively express their existing interest in and respect for human-animal relationships is a *missed opportunity* in domestic violence policy making, programming, and service provision. It misses the opportunity to allow workers to make connections in and between animal abuse and domestic violence, and reach victims living in high-risk situations. It misses the chance to reach victims stuck in violent households because of a lack of availability of alternative accommodation where humans and animal companions can reside together. And it fails to appreciate the important protective, connective, and healing work that human and animal victims can do for each other before and post-separation from violent perpetrators.

Illustrative Practice Examples

Throughout this book we have reiterated the likelihood of victims of domestic violence suffering immediate but also ongoing, if not lasting, effects. Our central arguments have been as follows: (1) the need to take animal victims of domestic violence seriously; (2) seeing violence done to animals in the home only or even mostly as a red flag for potential human-human abuse denies and demeans the experiences of animal victims; which (3) further marginalises, if not invisibilises, animals and, in turn, the many humans who love them and cannot leave violent homes without them. Earlier in this chapter we described some of the activities of the National Link Coalition. Several other community-based projects across the world are also advancing this work. Below is a selection of them.

RedRover: Bringing Animals from Crisis to Care (US)

Based in Sacramento, *RedRover* has been operating since 1987, comprised of some paid staff but an estimated 5000 volunteers across 50 states, who assist animals and people in crisis, and support providers of animal well-being programmes. An important part of their work is to offer financial help to human victims of domestic violence to escape and rebuild their lives with their animal companions. These include the following:

> Safe Escape grants: pay for temporary boarding and/or veterinary care to enable domestic violence victims to remove their pets to safety. For safety reasons, the application must be submitted by a shelter worker.
>   Safe Housing grants: fund start-up costs for domestic violence shelters seeking create a program to allow families and pets to escape abuse together. [They] … can help to build pet housing at the domestic violence shelter or help domestic violence shelters work with partners in the community to offer other pet housing options.

RedRover also contributes to SafePlaceforPets.org, which is an online directory of pet support programmes for pet owners facing domestic violence.

Safe Havens (US)

Across the US, safe havens involve a diverse range of community-based services that assist human victims of domestic violence to temporarily relocate their companion animals while seeking safety. The Safe Havens Mapping Project literally involves mapping the national network of foster carers, kennel space, pet-friendly refuge accommodation, and so on (Animal Welfare Institute 2018).

Lucy's Project: Safe Families—Paws and All (Australia)

Lucy's Project started in 2013 after Anna Ludvik gave birth to her still-born daughter Lucy. Anna sought to honour Lucy's death by creating a positive legacy. The organisation is founded on the belief that

> we fail to save human domestic violence victims lives when we fail to address the whole family- paws and all.... We recognize the trauma inflicted when beloved animals are abused as punishment, as a threat or means of control.... We recognize the role of many different fields and professions in responding to the intersection of companion animal ownership and domestic violence including vets, doctors, animal welfare organisations, crisis response systems, police, refuges, housing bodies, transitional homes and government ... that working together as a coordinated network is imperative to the overall goal of saving lives, improving the quality of life for survivors.

Lucy's Project operates as a peak organisation in Australia for linking practitioners and researchers addressing domestic violence and animal abuse, creating networks, holding conferences, sharing information and contacts, advocating for law reform, and educating the domestic violence sector about the involvement of animals. This includes supporting several women's refuges to transform their accommodation to become pet-friendly.

My Saving Grace (Australia)

Three people simply introduced as Lisa, Rich, and Kim started *My Saving Grace*, after a woman they knew used the term to describe the help her cat gave her to rebuild her life after domestic violence. They sought a way to engage people in the confronting topic of domestic violence, and the impact it can have on animals. Based on 'The Link' (between human and animal abuse) and other scholarly material about domestic violence, this project uses a mix of carefully crafted media, inclusive of personal testimonies to engage viewers in an exploration of

> the impact of domestic violence on companion animals and the people who love them, animal guardians, veterinarians, animal welfare workers, police, advocates, everyday people who believe that loving and protecting animals creates a safer and more connected world for everyone. (My Saving Grace, http://www.mysavinggrace.org.au/index.html)

Originally, they planned for the project to last six weeks. It has now been three years that they have been trying to change the story told about domestic violence, to include companion animals.

RSPCA Pets in Crisis and Safe Beds for Pets (Australia)

Across Australia there are several animal foster care projects supported involving the RSPCA and domestic violence services such as *Pets in Crisis* (Qld). An important benefit identified by *Pets in Crisis* (RSPCA 2018, n.p.) is that the programme "provides women with a release from their 'hostage' situations and enables families to seek refuge". For *Safe Kennels DV Project* (South Australia), the main objectives are also to collaborate with domestic and family violence organisations to ensure the safety of pets by offering emergency kennel accommodation and animal foster care. Two other important goals are to "[e]xplore the potential and where possible support initiatives for pets to remain with women and children escaping domestic violence from the outset" and "[a]dvocate for an increase in pet friendly rental accommodation". In Tasmania there is the *Safe Beds for Pets* programme which acknowledges that "[t]he safe beds program is not a long-term solution to the housing of the pet, but it gives domestic violence victims peace of mind and allows them to secure their own safety and make arrangements for the future" (RSPCA Tasmania 2016, n.p.).

The aforementioned examples are just a few of the many programmes and projects offering different responses to animals and humans caught in domestic violence. It is heartening that there are so many underway or in development, but it also a sobering reminder of the scale of the problem across the world.

Meeting the Needs of Companion Animals

Donaldson and Kymlicka (2015, 51–2) outline six broad commitments to meeting animals' needs. While their focus is on different species—on animals living in farmed animal rescues—we believe these commitments, with a slight modification, also apply to companion animals:

1. *Duty of care.* Provide a safe, healing environment for animals who have been abused by humans. Put the needs and safety of animal residents first.
2. *Support for species-typical flourishing.* Provide an environment that allows animal residents to engage in a range of behaviours and activities considered natural for members of their species.
3. *Recognition of individuality.* Appreciate animals as unique personalities, with their own needs, desires, and relationships.
4. *Non-exploitation.* Challenge conventional ideas about domesticated animals existing to serve human needs. Eschew use, sale, or other commercial activity involving animals.
5. *Non-perpetuation.* Prioritise existing animals rather than breeding new animals. Dedicate resources to rescuing animals already in existence.
6. *Awareness and advocacy.* Educate the public about animal sentience, animal cruelty, and abuse.

Our interpretation and application of these practice framework possibilities include encouraging others to use ideas from intersectionality, inclusive of speciesism, as a frame for understanding human-companion animal relations. While we appreciate the challenges, including the divisions that can exist among people who identify as 'animal lovers,' we are suggesting that we collectively step into, rather than away from, ethical questions about animal well-being and rights. A good place to start is to challenge the idea that humans are naturally superior to animals—and that this entitles humans to treat them as they see fit—as this is the kind of hierarchical thinking that supports domestic violence and allows it to flourish. Appreciating that companionate animal relationships with humans are not unilateral or unidirectional, nor should they be seen as such, means not naively celebrating the benefits that companion animals can offer to humans, but thinking about their needs and preferences as well as our own.

We all need to think through questions about the potential domination of and servitude still expected from some animal companions—and not just as a theoretical abstraction. This can involve observing subtle and/or overlooked behaviours, such as humans expressing annoyance when companion animals instigate contact during a time when they are busy with other activities. Is this annoyance the default position to animal-initiated communication? Are we open to putting down what we are doing and attending to their needs, not just if they are 'naughty' or somehow transgressive to human conventions but simply when they want to communicate with us at that moment? If we are rarely, if ever, prepared to do this, what does this say about our attitude of power towards them? Other associated questions include, but are not limited to, asking how we are responding to species-specific behaviours, such as dogs sniffing bottoms or rolling in mud, cats climbing up onto high places, or chickens pecking at freshly broken ground? What provisions are being made for the animals to (literally) express their voices, such as through barking, cat crying, and rooster and hen clucking? What opportunities do they have to express themselves physically and have contact with the earth, plants, natural smells, and toileting places? It is important to extend these kinds of questions beyond the biomedical and/or physical to ask about animals' emotional well-being—are they happy? Do they seem content? If they are traumatised, post-abuse, how can we help them recover?

Are they expected to always positively receive humans' advances, in spite of whether they are eating, sleeping, or feeling unwell? It is simply not fair to expect companion animals to be ever-available to their humans. This means recognising the work they perform and their needs as workers, for sufficient time off duty where they do not have to be hyper-vigilant to others' needs. It also includes monitoring workplace programmes involving companion animals to ensure that they are not just meeting the needs of the humans involved. Appreciation needs to be given to the risks associated with informal arrangements of humans bringing untrained and uncertified animals to visit public organisations. There are the potential risks to animals and humans, and also to insurance coverage. Employing the services of a reputable, positive-training visiting service, such as *Delta Therapy Dogs*, is preferable to ad hoc, informal arrangements.

More specific to the field of domestic violence, we must look beyond animals as 'red flags' for future violence humans inflict on other humans. We must ask critical questions about the propensity for companion animals to be hurt by domestic violence and think about what they might need to recover. Different modes of practice (such as research, social policy, community work, group work, and casework) can all be used to advance our knowledge of how animals may be affected in domestic violence, including times when they are helping humans to recover.

Conclusion

Throughout this book we have paid attention to the needs and experiences of companion animals caught up in domestic violence, explaining that to do otherwise—such as fixating on the potential benefits companion animals can deliver to humans—is to reproduce speciesism. In this last chapter we have discussed some of the historical development of frameworks, policies, and practices relating to domestic violence service provision to provide further context to our argument to include non-human animals in domestic violence conceptualisations, responses, and practices. We then made the case for recognising companion animals' work and well-being by building them into our theories, methods, and services—not as lesser beings or objects but as distinct individuals in their own right, complete with different personalities, preferences, and proclivities. Encouraging the recognition and valuing of emotional labour that animals do with/for their humans, we have emphasised the work they do during their time in violent households and post-separation.

We hope that this book has provided a sense of the importance of companion animals to some of those experiencing domestic violence and that it has drawn attention to the experiences of animals' themselves along with making it clear that, during crisis and recovery, animals and humans can help each other. Integrating this knowledge into policy, theory, and services is crucial to helping humans and their animals escape domestic violence. We also hope that this book has given strength to those who might be experiencing domestic violence, as well as to those who work at the frontline of support. Finally, we hope that we have encouraged people already working in domestic violence and related fields to think about ways to advance agendas of interagency collaboration that recognise the links between human and animal abuse so that humans and companion animals can stay together to support each other.

References

Alexander, R. (1993). Wife-battering – An Australian perspective. *Journal of Family Violence, 8*(3), 229–251.

Allen, K., Blascovich, J., & Mendes, W. B. (2002). Cardiovascular reactivity and the presence of pets, friends, and spouses: The truth about cats and dogs. *Psychosomatic Medicine, 64*(5), 727–739.

Amiot, C., Bastian, B., & Martens, P. (2016). People and companion animals: It takes two to tango. *Bioscience, 66*(7), 552–560.

Animal Welfare Institute. (2018). *Safe Havens Mapping Project for pets of domestic violence.* https://awionline.org/content/safe-havens-mapping-project-pets-domestic-violence-victims

Ascione, F. R., Weber, C. V., Thompson, T. M., Heath, J., Maruyama, M., & Hayashi, K. (2007). Battered pets and domestic violence: Animal abuse reported by women experiencing intimate violence and by nonabused women. *Violence Against Women, 13*, 354–373.

Banks, M. R., & Banks, W. A. (2002). The effects of animal-assisted therapy on loneliness in an elderly population in long-term care facilities. *The Journals of*

Gerontology Series A: Biological Sciences and Medical Sciences, 57(7), M428–M432.

Breiding, M. J., & Armour, B. S. (2015). The association between disability and intimate partner violence in the United States. *Annals of Epidemiology, 25*(6), 455–457.

Briefer, E., & McElligott, A. (2013). Rescued goats at a sanctuary display positive mood after former neglect. *Applied Animal Behaviour Science, 146*(1), 45–55.

Bunting, L., Lazenbatt, A., & Wallace, I. (2010). Information sharing and reporting systems in the UK and Ireland: Professional barriers to reporting child maltreatment concerns. *Child Abuse Review, 19*, 187–202.

Cancian, F., & Oliker, S. (2000). *Caring and gender.* Walnut Creek: AltaMira Press.

Cheers, B., Binell, M., Coleman, H., Gentle, I., Miller, G., Taylor, J., & Weetra, C. (2006). Family violence: An Australian Indigenous community tells its story. *International Social Work, 49*(1), 51–63.

Corvo, K., & Johnson, P. J. (2003). Vilification of the "batterer": How blame shapes domestic violence policy and interventions. *Aggression and Violent Behavior, 8*(3), 259–281.

Coulter, K. (2016a). *Animals, work, and the promise of interspecies solidarity.* New York: Palgrave Macmillan.

Coulter, K. (2016b). Beyond human to humane: A multispecies analysis of care work, its repression, and its potential. *Studies in Social Justice, 10*(2), 199–219.

Coulter, K. (2016c). Humane jobs: A political economic vision for interspecies solidarity and human–animal wellbeing. *Politics and Animals, 2*(1), 67–77.

Coulter, K. (forthcoming). Horses' labour and work-lives: New intellectual and ethical directions. In J. Bornemark, U. von Essen, & P. Andersson (Eds.), *Horsecultures: Ethical questions.* Routledge.

Crockett, C., Brandl, B., & Dabby, F. C. (2015). Survivors in the margins: The invisibility of violence against older women. *Journal of Elder Abuse & Neglect, 27*(4–5), 291–302.

Donaldson, S., & Kymlicka, W. (2015). Farmed animal sanctuaries: The heart of the movement? *Politics and Animals, 1*(1), 50–74.

England, P., Budig, M., & Folbre, N. (2002). Wages of virtue: The relative pay of care work. *Social Problems, 49*(4), 455–473.

Every, D., Smith, K., Smith, B., Trigg, J., & Thompson, K. (2017). How can a donkey fly on the plane? The benefits and limits of animal therapy with refugees. *Clinical Psychologist, 21*(1), 44–53.

Flynn, C. P. (2000). Woman's best friend: Pet abuse and the role of companion animals in the lives of battered women. *Violence Against Women, 6*(2), 162–177.

Fook, J. (2014). The meaning of animals in women's lives: The importance of the 'domestic' realm to social work. In *Animals in social work* (pp. 18–31). London: Palgrave Macmillan.

Frances, V., & Frances, A. (1976). The incest taboo and family structure. *Family Process, 15*(2), 235–244.

Fraser, H. (2008). *In the name of love: Women's narratives of love and abuse.* Toronto: Women's Press/Canadian Scholars Press.

Friedman, E., Son, H., & Tsai, C. C. (2010). The animal/human bond: Health and wellness. In A. Fine (Ed.), *Handbook on animal-assisted therapy: Theoretical foundations and guidelines for practice* (pp. 85–107). Oxford: Academic Press.

Hamilton, L., & Taylor, N. (2013). *Animals at work: Identity, politics and culture in work with animals.* Boston/Leiden: Brill.

Hamilton, L., & Taylor, N. (2017). *Ethnography after humanism: Power, politics and method in multi-species research.* London: Palgrave.

Headey, B. (1999). Health benefits and health cost savings due to pets: Preliminary estimates from an Australian national survey. *Social Indicators Research, 47*(2), 233–243.

Herd, P., & Meyer, M. (2002). Care work: Invisible civic engagement. *Gender & Society, 16*(5), 665–688.

Holt, S., Buckley, H., & Whelan, S. (2008). The impact of exposure to domestic violence on children and young people: A review of the literature. *Child Abuse & Neglect, 32*(8), 797–810.

Hovorka, A. (2015). The gender, place and culture Jan Monk distinguished annual lecture: Feminism and animals: Exploring interspecies relations through intersectionality, performativity and standpoint. *Gender, Place & Culture, 22*(1), 1–19.

Humphreys, C. (2007). Domestic violence and child protection: Exploring the role of perpetrator risk assessments. *Child & Family Social Work, 12*, 360–369.

Jewkes, R. (2002). Intimate partner violence: Causes and prevention. *The Lancet, 359*(9315), 1423–1429.

Kelly, L., & Westmarland, N. (2016). Naming and defining 'domestic violence': Lessons from research with violent men. *Feminist Review, 112*, 113–127.

Krug, E. G., Dahlberg, L. L., Mercy, J. A., Zwi, A. B., & Lozano, R. (Eds.). (2002). *World report on violence and health.* Geneva: World Health Organization.

Long, D. D., Long, J. H., & Kulkarni, S. J. (2007). Interpersonal violence and animals: Mandated cross-sector reporting. *Journal of Sociology & Social Welfare, 34*(3), 147–164.

Lucy's Project. https://lucysproject.com/

McKay, M. (1994). The link between domestic violence and child abuse: Assessment and treatment considerations. *Child Welfare, 71*(1), 29–39.

McMillan, F. (2017). Behavioral and psychological outcomes for dogs sold as puppies through pet stores and/or born in commercial breeding establishments: Current knowledge and putative causes. *Journal of Veterinary Behavior: Clinical Applications and Research, 19*, 14–26.

Michau, L., Horn, J., Bank, A., Dutt, M., & Zimmerman, C. (2015). Prevention of violence against women and girls: Lessons from practice. *The Lancet, 385*(9978), 1672–1684.

Morley, C., & Fook, J. (2005). The importance of pet loss and some implications for services. *Mortality, 10*(2), 127–143.

Morrison, M. L. (2007). Health benefits of animal-assisted interventions. *Complementary Health Practice Review, 12*(1), 51–62.

My Saving Grace. (n.d.). *The link between domestic violence and animal abuse.* http://www.mysavinggrace.org.au/index.html

Nancarrow, H. (2006). In search of justice for domestic and family violence: Indigenous and non-Indigenous Australian women's perspectives. *Theoretical Criminology, 10*(1), 87–106.

National Link Coalition. (n.d.). *Working together to stop violence against people and animals.* Retrieved September 24, 2018, from http://nationallinkcoalition.org/

Nicholas, R. F., & Gullone, E. (2001). Cute and cuddly and a whole lot more? A call for empirical investigation into the therapeutic benefits of human–animal interaction for children. *Behaviour Change, 18*(2), 124–133.

Nixon, J., & Humphreys, C. (2010). Marshalling the evidence: Using intersectionality in the domestic violence frame. *Social Politics, 17*(2), 137–158.

Pachana, N. A., Ford, J. H., Andrew, B., & Dobson, A. J. (2005). Relations between companion animals and self-reported health in older women: Cause, effect or artifact? *International Journal of Behavioral Medicine, 12*(2), 103.

Perryman, S. M., & Appleton, J. (2016). Male victims of domestic abuse: Implications for health visiting practice. *Journal of Research in Nursing, 21*(5–6), 386–414.

Petersen, M. L., & Farrington, D. P. (2007). Cruelty to animals and violence to people. *Victims and Offenders, 2*, 21–43.

RedRover: Bring Animals from Crisis to Care. (n.d.). *What we do.* https://redrover.org/what-we-do/

Renzetti, C. M., & Miley, C. H. (2014). *Violence in gay and lesbian domestic partnerships.* London: Routledge.

Riggs, D. W., Taylor, N., Signal, T., Fraser, H., & Donovan, C. (2018). People of diverse genders and/or sexualities and their animal companions: Experience of family violence in a bi-national sample. *Journal of Family Issues,* online first, https://doi.org/10.1177/0886260518771681.

Risley-Curtiss, C. (2010). Social work practitioners and the human – Companion animal bond: A national study. *Social Work, 55*(1), 38–46.

RSPCA (Queensland). (2018). *Pets in crisis.* http://www.dvconnect.org/pets-in-crisis/

RSPCA (Tasmania). (2016). *Safe beds for pets.* http://www.rspcatas.org.au/what-we-do/safe-beds-for-pets

Ryan, T. (2011). *Animals and social work: A moral introduction.* London: Palgrave Macmillan.

SBS. (2016). Hensioners and the power of therapy animals. *The Feed.* Retrieved June 24, 2018, from https://www.sbs.com.au/news/the-feed/hensioners-and-the-power-of-therapy-animals. Accessed 20 Aug 2018.

Scholtmeijer, M. (1996). The power of otherness: Animals in women's fiction. In C. Adams & J. Donovan (Eds.), *Animals and women: Feminist theoretical explorations.* Durham: Duke University Press.

Signal, T., & Taylor, N. (2008). Propensity to report intimate partner violence in Australia: Community demographics. *Behavior and Social Issues, 17*(1), 8–19.

Skeggs, B. (1999). Seeing differently: Ethnography and explanatory power. *Australian Educational Researcher, 26*(1), 33–53.

Spivak, G. (1988). Can the subaltern speak? In C. Nelson & L. Grossberg (Eds.), *Marxism and the interpretation of culture* (pp. 271–313). Basingstoke: Macmillan Education.

Stöckl, H., March, L., Pallitto, C., & Garcia-Moreno, C. (2014). Intimate partner violence among adolescents and young women: Prevalence and associated factors in nine countries: A cross-sectional study. *BMC Public Health, 14*(1), 751.

Swanson, R. W. (1984). Battered wife syndrome. *Canadian Medical Association Journal, 130*(6), 709–712.

Swanston, J., Bowyer, L., & Vetere, A. (2014). Towards a richer understanding of school-age children's experiences of domestic violence: The voices of children and their mothers. *Clinical Child Psychology and Psychiatry, 19*(2), 184–201.

Taft, A., Hegarty, K., & Flood, M. (2001). Are men and women equally violent to intimate partners? *Australian and New Zealand Journal of Public Health, 25*(6), 498–500.

Taylor, S. (2017). *Beasts of burden: Animal and disability liberation.* New York/London: The New Press.

Taylor, N., Fraser, H., & Riggs, D. W. (2017). Domestic violence and companion animals in the context of LGBT people's relationships. *Sexualities*, online first. https://doi.org/10.1177/1363460716681476

Victorian Government, Rent Fair Victoria: Pets are Welcome. Retrieved September 24, 2018, from https://www.vic.gov.au/rentfair/pets-are-welcome.html

Walsh, F. (2009). Human-animal bonds I: The relational significance of companion animals. *Family Process, 48*(4), 462–480.

Zasloff, R. L., & Kidd, A. H. (1994). Attachment to feline companions. *Psychological Reports, 74*(3), 747–752.

Zilney, L. A., & Zilney, M. (2005). Reunification of child and animal welfare agencies: Cross-reporting of abuse in Wellington County, Ontario. *Child Welfare, 84*(1), 47–66.

Index[1]

A

Advocacy, 85, 200, 209
Animal abuse
    exposed to domestic violence, 9, 133
    further risks post-separation, 44, 135, 174, 201, 205, 212
    targeted, 9, 33, 44, 49, 99, 108, 124, 129, 149
Animal companions
    emotion work, 23
    needs and welfare, 17, 22, 23, 42, 99, 124, 138, 145, 148, 159, 179, 196, 197, 210
    recovery, 22, 99, 127, 179, 195, 197
    speciesism, 209
    as victims, 17, 22, 23, 32, 60, 94, 99, 128, 143, 144, 155, 159, 195, 202, 205, 206

C

Care work
    and animals, 197
    and women, 194, 195
Cats
    emotional work of, 21
    impact of domestic violence on, 9, 128–138, 140, 141
    reactions to domestic violence, 141
    sensitivity to human victims/ survivors' needs, 22, 34, 60, 97
Children
    being soothed by animals, 10, 71, 111, 178, 195
    caring for animals, 104, 144, 176, 204
Class, 5, 6, 21, 39, 42, 43, 45, 59, 62, 98, 192–194
    importance of material concerns, 39, 192

---

[1] Note: Page numbers followed by 'n' refer to notes.

© The Author(s) 2019
N. Taylor, H. Fraser, *Companion Animals and Domestic Violence*, Palgrave Studies in Animals and Social Problems, https://doi.org/10.1007/978-3-030-04125-0

Coercive control, 109, 112–116, 163, 174

Companion animals
duty of care, 209
more than the benefits they can provide to humans, 4
programs to support those affected by domestic violence, 83, 201
See also Animal companions

Connections
with animals, 14, 15, 101, 104, 125, 200
with service providers who understand companion animal connections, 14, 15, 34, 204

D

Dogs
emotional work of, 21
impact of domestic violence on, 128–142
reactions to domestic violence, 174
sensitivity to human victims/ survivors' needs, 22, 34, 60, 97

Domestic violence
and animals, 4, 8, 13, 32, 35, 44, 60, 63, 64, 66, 67, 73, 77, 78, 80, 81, 125–128, 146, 207
and dogs, 8, 41, 96, 102, 104, 106, 107, 111, 114, 124, 128, 130, 132, 133, 144, 145, 149
effects on animals, 5, 22, 60, 124, 128–142, 146, 148, 149, 193, 208
effects on humans, 22
personal stories about, 7, 35, 63, 64, 66, 74, 108, 162, 208

policies and programs, 23
a political problem, 62, 63
services, 9, 34, 144, 145, 161, 165, 166, 180, 208, 211

E

Emotional labour, 83, 95, 98, 111, 139, 194, 196, 212
recognition of companion animals' work, 98, 211, 212

Empathy
empathic connection, 5, 96, 97, 131, 141, 146
empathic love, 4, 5, 22, 93–117, 174, 194

Escape, 22, 23, 42, 63, 94, 117, 126, 128, 144, 155–180, 200, 206, 212

F

Family
animals as, 22, 37, 100, 101, 109, 127, 197
growing up with animals, 100, 104, 106

Feminist intersectionality, 5, 29, 35, 38, 45–47, 67, 192–198
and animals, 29, 35, 46, 192–198

G

Gender, 5, 6, 17, 21, 38, 39, 42, 43, 45–47, 59–61, 72, 81n3, 97, 98, 106, 127, 190, 192–194
feminist intersectionality, 5, 45–47, 193, 194

Getting help

not as easy at it sounds, 93, 132,
147
recognising companion animals as
significant others, 49, 211

H
Housing
importance of, 8, 23
motel living, 165, 166
pet-friendly accommodation, 101,
131, 160, 180, 202, 207

I
Interspecies alliances, 4, 7, 22, 39,
95–96, 99, 100, 194–198
Interspecies solidarity, 197, 198
See also Interspecies alliances

K
Kin
animals as, 190

L
The link
animals as domestic violence
victims, 111, 138, 192
domestic violence and animal
abuse, 4, 8, 13, 17, 32, 35, 44,
49, 60, 64, 79, 128, 202, 205,
207
Love
coexisting with abuse, 29, 40, 42,
108, 194
empathy, 4, 5, 22, 23, 93–117,
131, 141, 155, 174, 194
loyalty and pain, 21, 29–50

M
Marginalised, marginalisation
invisibility, 206
of the work by subordinates, 68
Methodology
including animals, 126
visual methods, 15, 67

P
Parenting, 168–174
Perpetrators of violence, 3, 19, 60,
69, 190

R
Rebuilding post-separation, 23
Recovery
rebuilding post-separation, 4, 60,
179
Refuge
short- and long-term, 3, 34
Relationships
interspecies, 4, 22, 95, 99, 100,
194, 198, 204
parental, 170
of sexual intimacy that become
abusive, 36
Rescue
not always innocent, 20, 36, 163
rebuilding post-separation, 4

S
Species
cats, stories about, 8, 20, 96, 99,
128, 130, 193, 204
dogs, stories about, 8, 20, 48, 49,
85, 96, 97, 124, 128, 129,
149, 193

Stories
of domestic violence, 69
of hope for the future, 40, 108
of love and empathy, 39, 69

T
Trauma
anxiety, depression, suicidality, 34
recovering from, 99, 124, 179

W
Women
domestic violence campaigning by
the women's movements, 6
heterosexuality, 6, 16, 17, 38,
59–62, 157, 158, 162, 168,
194

CPSIA information can be obtained
at www.ICGtesting.com
Printed in the USA
LVHW071141251021
701442LV00006B/332